CELEBRITY CHEFS

Rachael Ray

Don Rauf

Enslow Publishing
101 W. 23rd Street
Suite 240
New York, NY 10011
USA

enslow.com

Published in 2016 by Enslow Publishing, LLC
101 W. 23rd Street, Suite 240, New York, NY 10011

Library of Congress Cataloging-in-Publication Data

Rauf, Don, author.
Rachael Ray / Don Rauf.
    pages cm. — (Celebrity chefs)
Audience: Age 12-up.
Audience: Grade 7 to 8.
Includes bibliographical references and index.
Summary: "Describes the life and achievements of TV personality and chef Rachael
Ray"— Provided by publisher.
ISBN 978-0-7660-7330-2
1. Ray, Rachael—Juvenile literature. 2. Cooks—United States—Biography—Juvenile
literature. I. Title.
TX649.R29R38 2016
641.5092—dc23
[B]
                                    2015029193

Printed in the United States of America

To Our Readers: We have done our best to make sure all websites in this book were
active and appropriate when we went to press. However, the author and the publisher
have no control over and assume no liability for the material available on those
websites or on any websites they may link to. Any comments or suggestions can be sent
by e-mail to customerservice@enslow.com.

Photo Credits: Cover, p.1 © Ap Photo; p.4 s_buckley/Shutterstock.com; pp.7, 20, 34,
40, 49, 54, 60, 63, 69, 85, 86, 95, 100 © AP Images; p.13 Aaron Davidson/Getty Images
for Food Network SoBe Wine & Food Festival; p.17 Yearbook Library; p.23 littleny/
Shutterstock.com; p.26 Milles Studio/Shutterstock; p.29 Philip Vaughan/ACE Pictures/
Newscom; p.31 Johnathan Esper/Shutterstock.com; p.37 AP Photo/The Post-Star, T.J.
Hooker; p.46 John Medina/WireImage/Getty Images; p.51 Brian Killian/WireImage/
Getty Images; pp.57, 83 © Food Network/Courtesy: Everett Collection; p.65 John Parra/
Getty Images; p.67 John Heller/WireImage/Getty Images; p.70 Ronna Gradus/KRT/
Newscom; p.75 s_bukley/Shutterstock.com; p.77 Tim Mosenfelder/Getty Images; p.79
Nicole DiMella; p.80 Sergi Alexander/Getty Images for SOBEWFF; p.89 Andy Kropa/
Getty Images; p.93 © King World Prod./Courtesy: Everett Collection; p.96 Official
White House Photo by Sonya N. Hebert; p.101 Mark Von Holden/Getty Images; p. 103
Thomas Klee/Shutterstock.com; p 104 Anna Shepulova/Shutterstock.com; p. 106 Olga
Miltsova/Shutterstock.com; p. 108 ©iStockphoto.com/Juanmonino; p. 110 Marysckin/
Shutterstock.com; p. 112 Joshua Resnick/Shutterstock.com; p. 115 ©iStockphoto.com/
Lauri Patterson.

CONTENTS

Rachael Ray

Small-Town Values,
Big Work Ethic

Rachael Ray, at five foot four, has always been a little dynamo. From a young age she was perky, talkative, and loud. On top of that, she has always had an incredibly strong work ethic—putting in longer hours than anyone else at every job she has ever had. Through hard work and her sheer exuberance, the woman who has always believed in small-town values has risen to become an internationally known celebrity, teaching people how to cook good food even if they have incredibly busy schedules. Her mission has been to show people that you can lead a rich life even if you are not rich—and she has shown audiences how to make the most of their time.

Her demonstrations on how to cook a meal in thirty minutes have made her a multimillionaire. As she stresses, she is not a professionally trained chef—she is just an everyday person who has trained herself how to cook really well. She's trying to show the rest of the world that they can do the same. Even Anthony Bourdain, the TV chef and commentator who can be critical of many celebrity chefs, has kind words about Ray. He explained in

The *New York Times* that she appeals to so many people because she is "a very recognizable, comfortable person, someone we all think we know, the sort of dream mom or sister we never had."[1] Every day, TV audiences tune in to see the woman who they see as family. With her infectious smile and laugh, she reaches people in their homes, encouraging them to take a bite out of life and say, "Yum-o!"

A Family of Hard-Working Cooks

Rachael Domenica Ray was born August 25, 1968 in Glens Falls, New York, to Elsa Scuderi and James Ray. Both sides of the family came from cultures with a rich appreciation of food. Elsa had an Italian heritage (from Sicily) and James was a Cajun from Louisiana with a Welsh, Scottish, and French background. Rachael has said that cooking is a way of life she was simply born into. "Everyone on both sides of my family cooks."

Rachael also has a brother Emmanuel or "Manny" born in 1974. She has a half-sister as well—Maria, Elsa's daughter from another marriage. Maria is eight years older than Rachael.

Ray credits Elsa, the oldest of ten children, with giving her such a strong work ethic. Rachael has said that she grew up attending the "School of Mama."[2] But she says her father, who worked in book publishing, had a unique gift for telling a story, and she has credited him with her ability to tell a tale. He also cooks Southern food, and Rachael learned about the spicy, bold cuisine of the South from him.

Ray always had a need for action and speed, her father in many ways believed in slowing down. Maybe his Southern roots led him to live in a more leisurely way. It took him three hours to cook a gumbo and six hours to grocery shop. Her brother, too, was the master of patience, and that may have helped him in

The keys to Rachael Ray's success are hard work, a love of food, and her down-to-earth personality. People relate to Ray because she admits she's not perfect and also because she knows how to make people comfortable. Her 30-minute meals are recipes that busy people appreciate.

---

his pursuit of mastering the martial arts. But dynamo Rachael had little patience. She was like the Energizer Bunny and Road Runner combined—she was tireless and wanted to move fast. In dance class as a child, she had trouble sitting still during the lecture portions—she just wanted to dance. No wonder she built a reputation around preparing meals in just thirty minutes. She has a need for speed.

As a child, Rachael saw what a speedy, busy life was like because of her family's involvement in the restaurant industry. They had owned and operated several restaurants called the Carvery in and around Falmouth and Mashpee, Massachusetts—part of Cape Cod. Both her parents worked in the restaurant biz when she was a young girl. At age eight, her family moved to upstate New York, to Lake Luzerne, which is very close to Lake George. Here, her mother managed nine restaurants in the upstate area, while her father left the food business and became the marketing director for a book publisher.

Rachael's mother had her helping in the kitchen as soon as she could hold a spoon. In her book *Rachael Ray's 30-Minute Meals: Comfort Foods*, Ray wrote, "I can remember being balanced on my mama's hip as she stirred big pots on the stove while in lively conversations with three different people. Then as now, food meant family, lots of good company, and happy moments together."[3]

For young "Rach," her connection to food was "burned" into her memory. Her earliest recollection was scorching her thumb on a griddle while using a spatula to scoop up some cheese. In *Good Housekeeping* August 2006, Rachael said, "My mom used to do this neat thing where she would take a piece of provolone or Swiss cheese, fry it up, then pinch the middle. We'd call them cheese bow ties. I loved them. But one day, when I was a toddler I was in a restaurant kitchen with her, and I saw a spatula. I thought, 'Oh, there's the thing Mom uses to make the cheese bowties, and I started to mimic her. Next thing you know, I had grilled my own thumb on the griddle."[4]

Her destiny in the food business seemed to be cemented the moment she spoke. Her family said that her very first word was "vino." She may have picked up the word from her mother, who frequently spoke Italian around the house. Or it may have come from her Italian grandfather who she says may have put wine diluted with water in her baby bottle to quiet her when she was fussy.

When she was twelve, she made her very first full meal all by herself. She cooked lasagna roll-ups with Gorgonzola cheese for her mom's birthday. She also remembers adding an artful touch by taking asparagus spears and fanning them out perfectly all around the plate. She made a "wine pairing" to go with it, which consisted of making a mimosa (a combination of champagne and orange juice). Already, Rachael Ray the chef was being born.

Childhood Shaped the Future Cook

One of Ray's most recognizable features is her deep raspy voice—a trait that she says came from having croup when she was a young girl. Croup is a loud cough that resembles the barking of a seal and is characterized by difficulty breathing. To treat her croup, the young Rachael had to inhale from a vaporizer. She constructed her own tent in her bed with a broomstick and sheet to keep the healing steam in.

In an interview with *Vanity Fair*, Elsa Ray remembers her daughter as a child who liked to be alone a lot, too.[5] She could be very quiet—writing or drawing for hours. Sometimes, she would get up in the middle of the night to draw and write in her self-made vaporizer tent.

And Mother Ray didn't mind if her kids were staying up late as long as they were being productive. If they wanted to get up and do something constructive—such as drawing, reading, or playing with an erector set to build a toy bridge—then she encouraged them to finish the project. They were allowed to stay up and work until they were exhausted and the work was done.

Rachael also had a lot of time to read when she was young. Her mother gave her one of her favorite books when she was just five or six. *The Casual Observer* by Elizabeth Whitson is about a curious girl who travels the world and asks a lot of questions to the people she meets along the way. In an interview in *Budget Travel* magazine[6], Ray said that one of her teachers once asked her to draw a picture of what she wanted to be when she grew up so she drew a picture of this weird little girl with a bonnet on. Her teacher wasn't clear on the drawing so asked, "So what do you want to be?" And Rachael said, "a casual observer!" "I always thought that it [a casual observer] was a real profession, but I think I became very much what I wanted to be," said Rachael.

Once a year, her mother would take her on a fun trip to New York City. They would visit the famous toy store FAO Schwarz or enjoy a Broadway show. From her trips to the Big Apple, she got a sense that something special would one day happen to her there. She felt she would return, and she had a feeling that New York would open some amazing doors for her.

The Driving Force of Mom and Gran'pa

Because her mother was the food supervisor of a restaurant chain, Rachael knew the food service industry well. Carl DeSantis owned the chain. Elsa opened restaurants, developed menus, and trained employees at nine locations. Elsa often brought her kids with her into the workplace because she didn't want strangers to watch them. She also didn't want them just sitting around as she worked so she put them to work in the kitchen.

"We did every crap job there was — dishwasher, busgirl," Ray has said in an article in *Good Housekeeping*.[7] She would sometimes work twelve-hour days in the kitchens. As she worked along with her mother, Rachael realized how hard her mother worked. Like Rachael, her mother has always been small but powerful. Elsa Ray stands about four-foot, eleven inches in high heels, but she is loud and fierce and has done the work of twelve men. Rachael has said that her mother would put in 100-hour workweeks but only get paid for forty hours. She always did the work that had to be done.

In the Food Network show *Chefography*, Ray explains how she has always worshipped her mother.[8] She says that her mother is simply better than her at cooking and decorating. If her mother had been born one-generation later, Rachael thinks she would have been a Food Network superstar. In *Forbes* magazine, Ray said that her mother taught her to work very seriously, but not to take herself too seriously.

In *Forbes* magazine, Rachael described her mother's philosophy: "Work harder than everyone else and never complain about it. Don't go to bed if you're not proud of the product of your day; stay awake until you are."[9] Ray says that her mother taught her to be grateful for every day and to have an adventurous spirit. She told Rachael to "take a left instead of the usual right on your way home from work, to talk to strangers, to make exotic dinners for yourself."[10]

Along the way, spending so much time either helping in professional kitchens or cooking at home, Rachael learned to cook as well. She said that neither her mother nor anyone else actually showed her cooking techniques—she just absorbed how to do it by being around professional chefs. Rachael also was interested in food when she visited local restaurants with her parents. When Rachael was a little girl she liked to go to a restaurant called Sutton's where she would crawl up on a stool and watch them make cider donuts. She love Montcalm Restaurant growing up, and she still goes back there. In particular, she loves the restaurant's Katherine Hepburn brownies, and she still gets them every year to celebrate her birthday.

> *"Work harder than everyone else and never complain about it. Don't go to bed if you're not proud of the product of your day; stay awake until you are."*

Mama Elsa is proud that all her children mastered some cooking skills—Maria is a good baker and Manny is a slow cooker. Rachael has always envied her sister's ability to bake. She claims, however, that she has gotten better at it over the years and can now make a decent éclair. Back when she was a kid, she tried to bake a cake for her mother's birthday. It took her four hours and she sifted the flour five times. She says the cake came out terrible, and she cried for three days. She and her sister did bond over cake, however. Sometimes they would buy a cake meant to be eaten by fourteen people, get in the car, and drive around town, taking bites until the entire thing was gone. Like many people with siblings, Rachael said that her brother and sister would often get on her nerves, and she would annoy them as well. But when all is said and done they have always loved each other and made each other laugh a lot.

Her grandfather—Elsa's father—Emmanuel was a big influence. He was a hard-working stonecutter (or stone mason) and passionate about food. He also had a deep joy for life. Some nights when he was a young man, he would wake his kids up and take them outside to see a beautiful star-filled night sky and sing them arias. He'd get up hours before daylight and cook meals for the family. To this day, Rachael makes a dish called Grandpa's Braised Beef, featuring Italian tomatoes and garlic, and Grandpa Emmanuel's Macaroni with Sausage and Cannellini. At holidays, she makes grandpa's special stuffed artichokes.

Food is in Rachael Ray's blood—her mother managed restaurants and her grandfather cooked Sicilian foods for the whole family. As a child, Ray appreciated foods that were different from what most American kids ate.

Emmanuel lived with the family when she was a small girl, and Rachael says that she was always at his feet. She says that she was his little rabbit. While other kids may have been eating more traditional American foods like hamburgers and hotdogs and meat loaf, she was eating the same diet as a Sicilian man in his seventies. She says that she loved the shredded, unsweetened wheat biscuits with coffee and cold milk he would eat for breakfast. She loved sardine sandwiches and stewed greens and anything with extra garlic and anchovies and chile peppers.

She carried her grandfather's influence with her into school. She couldn't stand the food at her school cafeteria because she was so spoiled by the home cooking. She was trained not to eat junk food. In *Good Housekeeping*[11] Ray said she would come home from school upset at first because the food was so terrible. She had never seen white bread before—it was something she couldn't stand. When she brought her lunchbox to school, she was a very unpopular little girl. She would bring the sardine sandwiches and rings of calamari that she would eat off her fingers. She also said in *People* magazine that her lunch made her reek of garlic so other students steered clear of her in the lunchroom. "I sat alone," she said in *People*. "but that's OK. I sat alone with good food."[12]

Both her mother and grandfather taught Rachael the importance of a hard day's work and how gratifying it feels to go to bed physically and mentally tired. Ray has also said that her grandfather gave her a good attitude. He told her that life can be good and life can be hard. But when life gets hard, you can either laugh or you can cry. He told her to not ever feel sorry for herself and to always laugh rather than cry because—it feels a whole lot better to laugh. "Being tired is good,"[13] Ray said in an interview on her website.

Her grandfather died when she was relatively young but she always remembers him fondly: "My grandfather was the funniest, coolest guy I've ever met. He knew a lot about everything and I lost him young. I've got so many questions for him now. And I think he would really love my dog—and my husband (in that order)! My husband's a lot like my grandfather, actually—both great gardeners and good eaters with a great sense of humor. And both tough guys!"[14]

A Split in the Family

In time, the relationship between James and Elsa became tumultuous. They were both taking antidepressants. Rachael admits that they were a family that would argue: "All of us have big tempers and love spicy food."[15] Eventually, they grew apart and divorced when Rachael was thirteen, according to *Good Housekeeping*. But Rachael said that her parents divorcing was actually a good thing. She said that most divorces are tumultuous, but in this case it was for the best. The relationship between her parents had become so fraught with fighting and anger that staying together was worse for them than being apart. "For us, it made for a happier family. It was miserable to watch people live together who shouldn't,"[16] Rachael said in *Good Housekeeping*.

And through the good times and the bad ones, one ingredient helped the family maintain stability, bond, and communicate: Food. Over meals, the family would share stories and talk about what was going on in their lives. Eating was a time to remember the anecdotes and family history. Food served as a bond for all the family members. When times were rough, Rachael and her family could always count on food to cheer them up.

Fitting In at School

As a young girl, Rachael joined the Girl Scouts; she swiftly earned demerits.[17] Girl Scouts just wasn't for her. She had a crazy streak of individualism that didn't fit well with being a Girl Scout.

High school, though, was a different story. Here, she fit right in. Through high school, the petite five-foot four-inch Rachael was brimming with energy and it seemed natural that she would be a well-liked cheerleader at Lake George High. She rallied her team, the Lake George Warriors, often climbing to the top of a cheerleader pyramid and doing a flip off the top and into the arms of her teammates.

Rachael had big-flying 80s hair, which was the fashion back then, and she always kept a can of hair spray in her locker. Her teachers remember her as one that other students wanted to be around. She was always thinking of something crazy to do. Teacher notes said that she was "extremely self-confident and unusually self-motivated. She always turned in quality work of the highest caliber. She's an unusually mature and responsible leader when she does not use people or resort to bossiness."[18] Rachael loved her high school and her experience there. Every year now, she returns to Lake George High School for an annual benefit cooking show that funds scholarships and district projects.

To cut loose in high school, she was like many other kids. She listened to KISS and she remains a fan of the band to this day. She said she'd go to parties like the other kids—hanging out in the woods listening to Led Zeppelin around a bonfire. Also, she had a big crush on the singer Tom Jones. Jones was known to send women into a fever with his gyrations. Her favorite song of his was "Delilah." Her childhood dream came true when Tom

It may come as no surprise to those who marvel at her high levels of energy that Rachael Ray (center) was a cheerleader at her upstate New York high school. Even now, Ray is a cheerleader of sorts for home cooks everywhere.

appeared with her on one of her TV shows. This was one of the few times she was flustered. She couldn't even look at him in the face she was so nervous.

Like many young people, she wanted to get her driver's license, but her first attempt at the driver's test is every teen's nightmare. During the exam, she drove over a cat and killed it. When that happened, she was so upset that she just got out of the car and left the driving test supervisor sitting there. Needless to say, she didn't pass on her first try, and she waited many

Cheerleading to
⭐ Success?

Like Rachael Ray, quite a few celebrity women started as cheerleaders, including Kirstie Alley, Meryl Streep, Alicia Silverstone, Kirsten Dunst, Paula Abdul, Cameron Diaz, Kelly Ripa, Fergie, Sandra Bullock, Lindsay Lohan, Jennifer Lawrence, Brooklyn Decker, Halle Berry, Megan Fox, Amy Poehler, Madonna, Diane Sawyer, and Katie Couric.

For Ray, cheerleading was particularly appropriate because she would go on to build an amazing career leading people with good cheer. Cheerleading meant so much to her that when she became famous she wrote a cookbook titled *Rachael Ray 2,4,6,8 Great Meals for Couples or Crowds*. The book was dedicated to cheerleaders everywhere. She said cheerleaders go beyond the girls with the pom-poms. This book was for the moms, dads, neighbors who watch our pets, water our plants, work two jobs, etc.

years before getting back behind the wheel and finally earning her license.[19]

The Budding Entrepreneur

Her family always saw her potential and thought she'd achieve great things, even when she was very young. Her father James called Rachael the hardest-working person he knows. Even as a child she had a touch of the showperson in her.

At one restaurant, she would hide behind the curtains at a huge picture window. She'd wait for diners to come in and take their seats. When they had settled in, she would jump from behind the curtain and surprise the diners with her big smile and a shout of "Hello, Buckaroos!"[20]

The young Rachael was also attracted to successful businesses and reached out to them. She wrote a letter to John Peterman, owner of the J. Peterman catalog to tell him how much she like his catalog and clothes. She titled her letter "Little Girl, Big Ideas." She once dreamed of opening a New Orleans-style jazz club in Saratoga, so she wrote Harry Connick Senior (father of current actor and musician Harry Connick Jr.) and asked him if his famous musician son would play a show in the city.

Her entrepreneurial spirit really took shape in high school when she started a business creating gift baskets of food. She named her enterprise Delicious Liaisons. She even wrote and designed her own catalog for the business. She ran the operation single-handedly, earning extra money selling her creations.

Along the way, she also waitressed at the local Howard Johnson's. Howard Johnson's, with its bright orange roof, was an iconic chain of diners that could be found throughout America in the 1960s and 1970s. Ray wore the standard-issue

Like many American high school students, Rachael Ray held a part-time job. She waitressed at the local Howard Johnson's restaurant, which, although they've nearly all closed now, were once mainstays across the country.

rusty orange-brown polyester uniform, and like many waitress uniforms it was hot and unbreathable. Ray was so short she had to jump deep inside the freezers to scoop up ice cream. Often her feet would go off the floor as she balanced with her stomach on the edge of the freezer. But she loved the work, and she loved interacting with customers.

Chapter 2

To the City
and Back

After graduating from high school in 1986, Rachael Ray had to decide what to do with her life. She was attracted to cooking and entrepreneurship with her gift basket business, but she knew those would be very hard roads to pursue with long hours. She also wanted to go to college and have the college experience. She was known as a talker and a good communicator, so she decided to head off to Pace University in Westchester, just north of New York City, and major in literature and communications.

Ray didn't feel very settled at Pace. She was exploring classes and searching, but she felt she wasn't finding the thing she was looking for. She kept up with her Delicious Liaisons business and she earned additional money by working various restaurant jobs. She described her time spent in college in *Vanity Fair*: "It was more like I was going to school for hobbies. I didn't know what I wanted to do."[1]

After two years, Ray realized she still didn't have a clear direction of what she wanted to do with her life. She was spending a lot of money on college and she didn't want that money to go to waste. So she made a decision. She would drop out of school, work and save money, and search for what she really wanted to do with her life. After she took some time to work and explore, then maybe she would return to school.

Ray set her sights on New York City. She always carried with her fond memories from her childhood visits. Like the lyrics in the song "New York, New York," she thought if she could make it there, she could make it anywhere.

In the early 1990s, she spotted a tiny ad in The *New York Times*. Macy's was looking for someone to work as a manager at its candy counter in its gourmet food cellar. Macy's was a famous New York department store with many branches across the United States. In the Food Network series *Chefography*, Ray recalled going into the job interview with Michael Corsello, who was a manager. Corsello saw that Ray only had experience working in small places upstate. He wasn't sure she was ready for the big time—Macy's. But she bowled over Corsello with the force of her personality. She told him how she was a super hard worker. She was fantastic with customers and she understood retail. In the interview, she was aggressive but funny. Corsello didn't need any more convincing. He was sold and hired the young Ray on the spot. The starting salary was about $24,000, but at the time, that was huge for her.

At Macy's candy counter, she was hard working and great with people. When a temporary position opened to be manager of the fresh foods department, she applied but was told she was "grossly under qualified." Still, she pushed for the job and Macy's decided to give her a shot. Corsello thought she would be in over her head, so he told her to just do the basics—write up schedules and make sure they were posted.

After deciding college wasn't for her, Rachael Ray found employment at the iconic department store Macy's, in the heart of New York City. Ray started in the store's famous gourmet food cellar, working at the candy counter. She quickly moved up the ranks.

Here, immersed in the world of good gourmet foods, she gained experience in everything from buying cheeses to shopping for Liza Minnelli's holiday food gifts. She learned about smoked salmon, pâté, caviar, the best olives, and more. She worked hard and absorbed as much as she could. Working with the best ingredients in the food world, she realized her passion. She wanted to work with food, but she still needed to find exactly how. To this day, Ray credits Corsello with getting her going in the food business. She said that he taught her everything about retail foods and a lot about business in general.

Macy's was impressed by the young dynamo, and soon they offered her a promotion. This time they asked her if she wanted to join the team in women's clothing and become an accessories buyer. She would be purchasing items like jewelry, hats, belts, and purses. But she didn't know anything about clothes. Plus, she just wasn't interested. Her passion was with food and that's where she wanted to stay.

The man who originally hired her had another offer. He was now working in Washington, D.C., and he invited her to work with him in retail food down there. The pay was excellent and the offer was tempting. But Ray was hesitant to leave New York City. She also had another major obstacle preventing her from taking the job: She would have to drive to work! She still didn't have a license after her upsetting episode running over the cat.

Moving on Up

In 1993, Ray heard of a new upscale gourmet food store called Agata & Valentina that was opening on the Upper East Side of Manhattan on the corner of First Avenue and 79th Street. Joe Musco named the store after his wife (Agata) and his daughter (Valentina). Musco was from a Sicilian heritage and he wanted

Some Random Facts
★About Rachael Ray

- **Favorite movies:** *The Godfather.* Anything with Will Ferrell, Vince Vaughn, or Jack Black. Westerns like *Unforgiven.* She also likes *Casablanca, An Affair to Remember, When Harry Met Sally,* and *There's Something About Mary*
- **Favorite kitchen appliance:** Food processor
- **Favorite sport:** Baseball
- **Favorite cookbooks:** All those written by Marcella Hazan
- **Food she hates:** Mayonnaise! (She says it creeps her out. Rachael has created many salad dressings and potato salad recipes that are mayo-free) [2]

to sell the best that Italy has to offer—homemade mozzarella cheese, sausages stuffed with pork, veal, cinnamon, garlic, lemon zest and currants, smooth ricotta gelato, olive oils, and fresh pastas. In Ray's interview with Musco and his family members, they bonded over their passion for food and their common Sicilian heritage. In fact, they had so much to talk about, the interview reportedly lasted nine hours.

As a manager at the store, Ray brought her "A" game and helped the store become a success. In *From Scratch: Inside the Food Network,* author Allen Salkin writes that Ray was ready and

Gourmet food markets like Agata & Valentina that sold fancy condiments, packaged products, and prepared foods had become popular in New York City beginning in the 1970s. Eventually these types of stores expanded across the country and brought a new level of sophistication to American cuisine.

able to perform just about any task from unsticking a troublesome cash register to repairing a meat slicer. She distinguished herself with outstanding customer service and by working harder than anyone else. She'd often wake at three o'clock in the morning at her apartment in Woodside, Queens, so she could get to the story early in the morning to receive deliveries.[3]

A Crime That Changes Everything

One night after working past midnight, Ray's boss drove her home and dropped her off. Two men were hanging out in the vestibule of her apartment, but Rachael was very trusting and didn't think anything of it. In an interview in *TV Guide*, she explained how she now realizes how dumb she was. She fumbled with her keys to get in the door to the building and kept apologizing to the two men that she was taking so long. Without warning, one of the young men flashed a pistol.

Some people would react to that situation by giving the criminal money, or crying, or pleading with them not to hurt her. Rachael, however, had the fighting spirit. She quickly reached in her bag for a little can of aerosol mace. Her dad had given it to her, and she always carried with her, attached to her subway token holder. Mace is an irritant that is similar to tear gas—it causes severe but temporary pain when sprayed in the face. Ray started screaming loudly and quickly sprayed one of the muggers in the face. He screamed with pain. The two assailants ran away quickly.

Ray called the police and they drove around the neighborhood in hope of finding the attackers, but they had no such luck. Ever the dedicated worker, Rachael went to bed after the incident, slept just a couple hours, and went right back to work the next day. "It was a very, very scary moment," Rachael has said in *TV Guide*. "And I probably should have left the city right then and there."[4]

A few days later, she was at work and she was sitting in a position that put her foot to sleep. When she got up quickly to answer a ringing phone, she fell over and broke her ankle. Now she was forced to hobble around on crutches. And she didn't have anyone special in her life to help her out—she had recently been through a bad breakup.

As if all of this were not bad enough, about ten days after the first mugging, one of the teenage assailants from the first attempted robbery returned. In *TV Guide*, Rachael said that she again was entering her housing complex when the boy appeared from nowhere. He stuck a weapon into her gut and dragged her into a passageway outside the building. She thought that the first failed mugging embarrassed the male and he was back to get revenge. The young man began to pistol whip her.

"He beat the crap out of me with his gun," Rachael recalled in *People* magazine.[4] Although bloodied and beaten, Rachael yelled for the building's guard dog. "Lisa! Lisa!" she screamed. She was looking up to see a gun pointed directly at her head. "That was it," she said in *TV Guide*. "I was pretty sure I was dead." But her calls to the dog worked, and Lisa came running. Although on a long chain, the dog bolted up the alley, barking loudly. The dog's barking was enough to chase off the criminal again. Rachael hobbled on her broken foot to get help and was taken to the hospital.

In the hospital, she made a decision. She had to leave New York. In *Vanity Fair*, Rachael said, "People have a lot worse things in life. But it was like, O.K., I'm not going to wait for strike three. I felt the whole universe was telling me, you're not supposed to be here right now."[6]

Although she enjoyed moderate success with her career, Ray endured a series of hardships that resulted in her leaving New York City. The event that triggered her departure was being badly beaten during a second attempted mugging. After that, Ray decided to pack it in.

> *"I felt the whole universe was telling me, you're not supposed to be here right now."*

While she felt this was the right decision and the best decision, it was also a very difficult one to make. She was young, energetic and leading a very successful life in New York City. But now she felt defeated. New York, which had held such promise for her, was a place she no longer wanted to be. New York was not magical at all— it was a dark and dangerous city and all she wanted was to get out and return to safety. She decided she would move back upstate and live with her mother and start over there. It would not be New York City but somehow she would carve out a career there.

Some warned her that she would never find the opportunities upstate that Manhattan had to offer, but she wanted to reconnect with her hometown roots. She called friends who helped to pack all of her belongings. She would not even go back to her apartment at all because she didn't want to go back to the scene of the crime. It was all too upsetting. With all her possessions packed, she headed north, some 200 miles, and moved back in with her mother in the woods of the Adirondacks.

While some would think this might have been the end of Rachael Ray's rise to success, it was really just the beginning. Ever the optimist, Ray now looks back at the violent episode and strangely sees the silver lining. In *TV Guide*, she said that if she had not been mugged, she would probably still be working as a buyer and manager at Agata & Valentina. The move upstate was actually propelling her closer to stardom.

After struggling in New York City, the clear air and beautiful landscape of upstate New York felt welcoming to Ray. She enjoyed the country life, as well as being closer to her family. She didn't know it then, but the move would also take her career in unexpected directions.

Chapter
3

Heading Home
to Success

Upstate in the Adirondacks, the countryside is filled with millions of acres of forests, mountains, streams, and many lakes. Rachael Ray has always thought that the Adirondacks, or "Dacks," is one of the most beautiful places on Earth. For her, it was the perfect environment to heal mentally as well as physically. Lake George is one of the jewels of the area, and it has been admired for centuries for its beauty. "Lake George is without comparison, the most beautiful water I ever saw..." wrote Thomas Jefferson. The artist Georgia O'Keeffe found great inspiration here, and she spent many summers painting along the lakeshores.

On these very shores at Bolton Landing, the historic, award-winning, five-star Sagamore Resort had been attracting vacationers since the 1880s. The resort still offers kayaking, sailing, swimming, hiking, golf, and other recreational activities. The resort also has a casual fun restaurant called Mister Brown's Pub. Rachael found this eatery especially inviting. The restaurant serves excellent food at modest prices. Dishes include lump crab cakes, roasted garlic hummus dip,

Gorgonzola steak salad, pecan-crusted trout, butter squash ravioli, and the Adirondack pub burger. In 1994, Rachael started managing the pub and found herself on the road to recovery.

A Cabin of Her Dreams

Shortly after moving back to the area, Ray also fell in love. She didn't fall for a man, but for a beautiful, small cabin situated about twelve miles away from her old high school. In the Food Network show *Chefography*, Ray described seeing the cabin for the first time as love at first site. She knew she had to live there. The cabin had an Italian country vibe and definitely was no-frills. It had linoleum in the kitchen, no dishwasher, and dirt under the wood floors. She paid $575 a month, which was a huge amount for her at the time. At this stage in her life, she was back to living paycheck to paycheck. The payment plan was a rent-to-own set-up, so in theory she would own the cabin one day.

She knew she had found an ideal home, and she, her mother, and sometimes her brother would live there on-and-off for years to come. The cabin would give Ray the peace and comfort she needed to try out and write recipes. This is where she would enjoy good food and a warm kitchen in the years to come. She believed in small-town values—this is what gave her strength and confidence. She may not have had much at this point in her life, but her mother taught her well—you can stretch your dollar and make the most of wherever you live. You can decorate and cook good food with any budget.

In *Good Housekeeping* magazine, Ray said of her mother: "Like a true Italian, she valued beautification in every area of her life, and I try to do the same. She raised me with a great aesthetic and taught me that you don't need to be rich to live a

Safely ensonced in the Adirondacks, Rachael Ray began managing Mister Brown's Pub, part of the five-star Sagamore Resort. Living a simpler life allowed her to reflect on her time in New York City and she began to set some goals.

rich life."[1] Ray didn't know it at the time, but this was a philosophy that she would be delivering to the entire country, and her passion for this approach to life would make her famous.

Although she was just getting by in the country, she had time to think, and when she thought back to her time in New York, she realized she was putting in 100 hours a week, but what was she really getting back in the end? "I thought I had this great life, but I had a lousy one," she said in *Good Housekeeping*. "If you're going to work that hard, it should be for something with your name on it."[2]

True, at this stage in her life, her name was not on anything. But she was now looking for that opportunity.

A Return to Gourmet Foods

In 1995, she heard of a position as a food buyer at a gourmet market in Albany, New York. The business was called Cowan

& Lobel, owned by Jay and Donna Carnevale. This was a great job, and it was similar to her positions with food at Macy's and Agata & Valentina. She liked gourmet food. And this type of job gave her a chance to interact with the masses. This type of environment was teaching her an amazing lesson—she was learning how real people shop and eat.

While the position seemed to be a natural match and one that would be a great step up for her, Ray had a major obstacle. At age 27, she still didn't know how to drive, and to get this job everyday, she would absolutely have to get behind the wheel of a car. The memory of her disastrous first driver's test—and the cat—still haunted her. But Rachael wasn't one to sit still. She had to move on to something that might lift her higher and earn her more money. She enrolled in driving lessons and after about three weeks, she took the driver's test and earned her license.

She bought an old Ford pickup and was ready for work. But her first day driving to work was still pretty nerve-wracking. Ray clutched the steering wheel with all her might to and from the job. To make matters worse, she was pulled over by a policeman on her drive home because she was driving with her high beam headlights on. Her Ford pickup was so new to her that she wasn't sure where her high beam switch even was. It took her a few minutes to figure out how to turn them off.

One day, not too long after she had begun, she swerved on the highway and flipped her truck. Even though that accident added to her list of traumas, Ray was not deterred. She had her mother drive her to work for a short period of time. She had to be at the store to receive foods that had to be refrigerated—if she wasn't there and the food did not go into the fridge, it would go bad, and she wasn't going to let that happen.

Although Ray had complained about working long hours in New York, she really couldn't help herself. It was her nature. She was simply a hard worker and she always put in the extra time to get the job done right. Vicky Filiaci was already working at Cowan & Lobel when Ray arrived on the scene. In *Vanity Fair*, Filiaci said that Rachael was a total workaholic: "Her first holiday there, the store was just amazing," she said. "It had never looked so good, and we'd never had so many cool things for our holiday. She bought it all, she put it all out, and it was just gorgeous stuff."[3]

In *Chefography*, Filiaci said that she and Rachael did not hit it off right away. Filiaci said that Ray came off as a bit of a know-it-all. They had a disagreement about how to prepare caponata, an Italian eggplant dish. They both had strong personalities and differences of opinion on food. Soon they found themselves screaming at each other over the caponata. Although hostility built up between the two, Ray was able to diffuse the situation by telling Vicki, "It's only eggplant!" After that they became very good friends.

Ray was busily working away as a buyer when in September of 1996, the chef who prepared all the takeout dishes quit. Ray enjoyed a challenge, and she really enjoyed cooking, so she asked her bosses if she could temporarily step into the position while they hunted for a new cook. She balanced her food buying responsibilities with the food preparation. Rachael's cooking was a hit with customers. The takeout meals were flying out the door. The owners of Cowan & Lobel asked her if she would work as both the chef for the store and the buyer. Ever the busy bee, Ray said yes.

At Cowan & Lobel, Ray started as a food buyer but eventually took on additional food preparation responsibilities. These positions taught her what people liked and didn't like to eat.

The Birth of the 30-Minute Meal

Donna and Jay Carnevale were pleased that Ray's cooking was a smash, but they noticed that many of the gourmet food items just weren't selling. Ray knew they were offering great products—she bought them after all, but she needed to find out why customers weren't purchasing. She started informally interviewing the shoppers. She asked them why they weren't buying groceries and why they weren't cooking. She heard the same answer again and again. People were too busy and had no time. They would rather just buy Rachael's prepared food and enjoy her delicious creations rather than take all the time required to cook.

Ray carefully thought over how she could change customer attitudes about cooking. At the time, Domino's Pizza had a campaign promising to deliver its pizzas within thirty minutes. She thought that if people were willing to wait a half hour for pizza, they should be willing to cook a meal if they could do it in thirty minutes.

Ray told the Carnevales that they should sell gift certificates for cooking classes called "30-Minute Meals." The classes would teach customers how to use foods to prepare delicious dinners, and they'd be able to do it all in a short amount of time. Cowan & Lobel would find professional local chefs to teach each class.

The Carnevales loved the idea. They decided to print up the certificates for the classes and sell them, and as they sold the certificates they would round up chefs to participate. The certificates were a hit with customers snatching them up. Finding the chefs, however, was not as easy as they thought. All the cooks they approached either wanted too much money or they didn't have the time. Donna Carnevale knew the solution: Rachael had to teach the classes. Ray resisted. She was not a professional chef. But Carnevale said that she made food that everyone loved. Plus, she was great with customers, and she had no trouble talking.

So Rachael took on a new role, and it would be a key step in her journey to becoming a super-popular TV host. In *American Profile*, she said she first created a packet of thirty 30-minute Mediterranean meals. At Cowan & Lobel the bestsellers were the pasta and chicken dishes. Each class Ray taught lasted about three hours. She would teach six basic recipes and five versions of what to do with each dish, so in that three hours you could really learn thirty 30-minute meals. "I taught the same things that I teach on my show," Rachael said in *American Profile*, "and that's how it started." [4]

In *Newsweek*, she described how she set up her first cooking station in the grocery store with whatever she could find. She described her ovens as "Easy Bake ovens on steroids." [5] She brought in her own pots and pans. She brought in apple crates for decoration and to move items around. They set up huge carts that held little mirrors. The mirrors were directed at her hands so customers could see her preparation techniques. In *Chefography*, Ray stresses that she wasn't showing customers official cooking approaches. She didn't know how to properly chop an onion. She would basically hack it to bits, but she would get the job done and get the meals made in thirty minutes. The bottom line was this: She didn't need to know official culinary techniques because she knew how to make great-tasting food and how to make it fast.

A Natural for TV

Word spread on her entertaining, fun classes. Wednesday nights at Cowan & Lobel were the place to be. Soon she had a wide range of people lined up to take her courses, including seniors, people planning to get married, football players, and even Girl Scouts.

As news traveled about Ray's popular, entertaining courses, Dan DiNicola heard about them and thought it would be interesting to check them out. DiNicola was a reporter working at the Albany TV station WRGB, Channel 6. He was skeptical that a person could really prepare a meal in thirty minutes. It seemed

One of Ray's best ideas at Cowan & Lobel was teaching a class on 30-minute cooking. She would parlay this to a similar show on the Food Network.

impossible. He told Donna Carnevale that he'd like to come to a class. He also told her that he didn't know how to cook at all. She told him to come that night and try it out. What he didn't tell any one was that he was bringing an entire camera crew. He filmed Rachael that night, and he was bowled over. The perky chef captivated him and he actually learned to cook a meal in just half an hour. He also was smitten with Rachael and they soon began dating.

DiNicola offered Ray a regular three-minute segment on the local news where she could present a fast cooking lesson. She was a natural on TV. With her big brown eyes, brown hair, and infectious smile, she was an attractive TV personality. And she knew how to talk and get people excited about food. Her presentation soon became titled "The 30-Minute Meal With Rachael Ray." She got paid about $50 a segment.

Off to Price Chopper

With low pay on local TV, Ray needed to keep working a Cowan & Lobel. However, when Donna Carnevale had a falling out with the family and quit, Rachael decided to follow. Rachael was taking Donna's side in the argument and sticking by her. She didn't have any other job lined up but she quit in allegiance to Carnevale. As so many of her friends would say throughout her life, Rachael was always loyal. That was one of her best qualities.

She's an equally dependable ally to new friends, too. Chef Mario Batali, who became her Food Network colleague, says Ray "will go the extra mile for anything I would ask of her." Her friends value not just her loyalty but also the wisdom she shares. Says Batali: "People think of her as just eye candy, but she is crazy business-savvy and really, really smart."[6]

It didn't take Ray very long to find a new gig. The local Price Chopper stores wanted some of the Rachael magic, and she was soon doing her cooking lessons for that chain. The local TV station where she had been doing her cooking segments decided to expand her airtime. One of the news directors asked her to do travel segments on the news. In her new feature called "Home and Away," she advised viewers how they could take fun vacations without breaking the bank. She was also taking her cooking show into people's homes and showing folks how to prepare fast meals in their own kitchens. By doing all these TV appearances, Ray became more and more comfortable on camera. She could ad-lib and teach and keep a lively time going through it all. And people were taking notice—she won two local Emmy awards for her work.

Start the Presses

People who came to the classes at Price Chopper jotted down notes and learned to cook in thirty minutes, but many wanted the recipes collected all together. Ray said she got angry letters from customers who said they couldn't find her recipes anywhere. So she gathered her recipes and collected them for publication in a book. She found a small, one-woman publishing house in New York—Lake Isle Press headed by Hiroko Kiiffner. Kiiffner had never heard of Rachael Ray. And she had seen ideas like hers before—cookbooks showing how to make meals in fifteen, twenty, and thirty minutes. Peter Franey, the acclaimed French chef, had put out a book titled *The 60-Minute Gourmet.* Well, in this fast-moving modern world, even sixty minutes was too long to cook.

Plus, Ray really didn't have an organized book ready to publish. All she had was basically a stack of recipes. She did, however, have a special selling point—she had already discussed the idea of a book with Price Chopper and they had agreed to carry it in their stores and sell it. With her charm, recipes, and a distribution plan, Ray sold Kiiffner on the idea and the publisher printed up several thousand copies in time for Christmas 1998. The book was so popular in Albany and the surrounding area that it sold 10,000 copies almost immediately. It only took three months before the book had to go into a second printing.

The book featured her top ten meals with fewer than ten ingredients, top ten kid's favorites, thirty-minute pastas, salads and other green stuff, thirty-minute comfort foods, and make your own take-out with burgers, Indian, and Asian choices. Her "Gran'pa Emmanuel" was represented with Emmanuel Nini's Ziti and Sausage Cannellini, Manny's Many–Herb Sauce With Walnuts, Manny's Sweet and Sour Sauce, and Sicilian Sausage and Fennel Pasta.

"That was the biggest achievement in my life at that point," Ray said. "I remember my mom and I got the check in January, and we danced through the streets and just thought it was the most money in the world ever. We went to a really great restaurant and bought nice dresses for ourselves and had the best time."[8]

Recipes Flow from "The Kitchen in My Head"

Kiiffner was sold on Ray and Ray liked Kiiffner. Again, a loyal bond was established, and Rachael would take her next nine cookbooks to Lake Isle Press to be published. Together, they would sell millions of copies. After her first nine books with Kiiffner, Ray moved on to publish her books with Clarkson Potter, an imprint of Random House. Ever loyal, however, she gave Kiiffner the rights to keep reprinting and selling the nine

The Top Ten
★30 Minute Meals

Based on requests after airing her cooking segments on WRGB, Rachael selected the top ten 30-Minute Meals overall[7]. Here they are:

Jambalaya: Quick Jambalaya

Puttanesca Pizza: Tomato, Onion, Caper and Anchovy

Super Sub Balls and Pig Skin Potatoes
(an ideal meal for Super Bowl Sunday)

The Real Deal—Yes, You Have to Use an Egg, No Mustard, Hold the Mayo, Caesar Salad

The Three R's: Rigatoni, Rapini, and Ricotta Salata Pasta

Taco Pockets

Moo Shu Pork Pockets with Jasmine Rice Sundaes

My Sister Ria's Favorite Fajitas

Curry in a Hurry

Emmanuel Nini's Ziti with Sausage and Cannellini.

titles they did together. By 2005, Ray had 4.5 million books in print, and she had signed a $6 million deal with Clarkson Potter.

Ray puts out three cookbooks in a year and they each sell a million copies. At least five of her books hit number one on the bestseller list. Over the years, the list of her top-selling titles piled up rapidly. Some of her popular books include *30-Minute Meals: Get Togethers, Comfort Meals, Veggie Meals, The Open House Cookbook, Cooking Round the Clock, Cooking Rocks! Rachael Ray 30-Minute Meals for Kids, Rachael Ray Best Eats In Town On $40 A Day, Rachael Ray 30-Minute Get Real Meals, Rachael Ray 365: No Repeats A Year of Deliciously Different Dinners, Express Lane Meals, Yum-o! The Family Cookbook.*

Later in 2012, she put out *Rachael Ray: My Year in Meals* with Atria Books, a division of Simon & Schuster. It was a food and drink diary of everything she and her husband and their friends and family ate and drank for year. Also that year, she published *The Book of Burger* with Atria. She started hosting an annual South Beach Wine and Food Festival and NYC Wine and Food Festival Burger Bash.

> *"The concept of 30-Minute Meals has become so ingrained in my very being that I write them in my sleep."*

She has put out so many cookbooks that people sometimes wonder if Ray will one day run out of recipe ideas. In her book *Just in Time*, she writes: "The concept of 30-Minute Meals has become so ingrained in my very being that I write them in my sleep. I keep notebooks on the bed stand whether I'm at home or traveling, for the 3 A.M. call from the kitchen in my head.

Ray capitalized on the success of her local 30-minute meal classes, collecting the recipes into a popular cookbook.

When I look at ingredients I see increments of time. When I walk through the grocery sore, I don't see red peppers and green beans. I see five to six minutes in a sauté pan, and two minutes in boiling salted water."[9]

And when the fans came out to see her, there was worship. Batali describes a Rachael Ray book signing like this: "At book signings and public appearances, I have seen her fans faint, tremble, mumble, moan and ultimately hit the front of the line and embrace their food hero, repeating her mantras such as 'let's run a knife through it' and 'easy peasy.'"[10]

Chapter

4

The
Perfect Storm

Things were going well with her small upstate empire, but Rachael Ray was ready to go up a level. As luck would have it, one day Lou Ekus was driving in upstate New York heading to the Culinary Institute of America. Ekus had been building a thriving a business teaching chefs how to present themselves on television.

Lou Ekus began his career as a director of prosthetics and orthotics dealing with artificial limbs and braces at the Shriner's Hospital in Springfield, Massachusetts. He would do publicity and media appearances for Shriner's. He made mistakes along the way but learned how to perform better in front of the camera. Then, he started working with a publicity firm that was sending cookbook authors on book tours.

In 1993, there was a major shift in the world of cooking when the Food Network launched in New York City. Up until this point, there had been some famous chefs who had gained success by appearing on television, such Julia Child and Graham Kerr (also known as the Galloping Gourmet). But this new cable network was featuring chefs who were showing the world how to cook around the clock.

By 2000-2001, the Food Network was hitting its stride, gaining viewers and making a few chefs into nationally recognized superstars. The New Orleans chef Emeril Lagasse had a wildly successful, top-rated program called *Emeril Live!* Bobby Flay had a few popular shows and in spring of 2000, he would compete on the hugely popular show *Iron Chef*, battling in out in "Kitchen Stadium" against Iron Chef Japan, Masaharu Morimoto. Ekus had spent time with Flay and Emeril giving them media training and helping them to be more natural and relaxed on camera. Ekus had done the same for Chef Ming Tsai, who had a Food Network show called *East Meets West*, and for Sara Moulton, who hosted *Cooking Live*.

Ekus knew what it took to be successful on TV, and he had an ear and eye for talent. When he pulled into the parking lot of the Culinary Institute, he was absolutely riveted by this woman who was being interviewed on the radio program *Vox Pop* on WAMC. He had never heard her before but she was natural, engaging, and fun. The woman was talking about her new cookbook, which was all about how to prepare meals in just thirty minutes. She was describing how to make a 30-minute jambalaya—a traditional Louisiana dish that was similar to paella and featured shrimp, chicken, and sausage. Of course, Ekus couldn't see Ray, but he was blown away by what he heard.

Ekus was so impressed he made a call immediately to Bob Tuschman, the Food Network's senior vice president of programming. He told Tuschman that he had to call him right away because he was hearing this amazing woman on the radio. He told Tuschman that she had a cookbook about 30-minute

New Orleans chef Emeril Lagasse had been one of the Food Network's earliest successes. He had the network's top-rated show, *Emeril Live!*, when executives called Rachael Ray.

meals, and he needed to track down this Ray woman and find out more about her.

According to Allen Salkin in the book *From Scratch*, Tuschman went directly to his bookshelves to see if the Food Network had a copy of Ray's cookbook. As fate would have it, the book was there and Tuschman saw the photo of a bright, young, energetic woman on the cover. He flipped through the book and liked the concept. These were recipes for regular folks who had no time to cook and were shopping at normal grocery stores, not upscale food markets. Tuschman had been looking for new talent for the Food Network—someone who could speak to a broader audience. He immediately saw potential for a TV show based on her concept. He took note of the publisher, Lake Isle Press, and called their offices. Tuschman reached Hiroko Kiiffner on the phone and asked if it were possible to set up a meeting with Ray.

In an interview with *Reality Wanted*, Tuschman said, "When she walked in the door, I thought she was filled with energy, fun and charisma and we basically signed her on the spot. I think star power is a combination of a lot of personality attributes. I think it starts with passion, energy, warmth, relatability, excitement, and charisma. Literally, there is a light in someone's eyes. I always equate it to when a person walks into a room and you can't take your eyes off of them. Rachael definitely had that. I felt that when I met Giada (De Laurentiis), her personality is so vibrant. I look for that vibrancy and that electricity in anyone I meet."[1]

A Game-Changing Appearance

Around this same time that the Food Network was becoming aware of Rachael, Al Roker had her on his mind as well. For

Food Network executive Bob Tuschman discovered Ray and hired her immediately. Previously, the network's programming had been dominated by acclaimed chefs. Tuschman believed viewers wanted easy recipes from a regular cook.

years, Roker has been the weatherman and one of the hosts on NBC's popular morning program the *Today Show*. He has a house in upstate New York, and he happened to see Ray on the local news there. Roker saw great potential in her, and thought she might be perfect for a segment on the *Today Show*. In early March of 2001, a gigantic late winter snowstorm was expected to hit New York City, and a lot of guests who were due to appear on the the *Today Show* were cancelling in advance of the anticipated blizzard.

A producer from The *Today Show* found the number to reach Ray's cabin upstate. She got her mother, Elsa, on the phone and asked if her daughter would like to do an appearance on the show with Al Roker. Elsa said she would track down her daughter right away and have her call back. Rachael was at a Price Chopper at the time doing one of her classic 30-minute meal prep classes. On her website, Rachael said she was in the meat department demonstrating how to cook meat-based dinners. The poster said: "Rachael Ray: She Knows Meat!" "My mom said, 'The 'Today' show just called you!" I said, "Oh, come on. It's somebody playing a joke on me."[2]

Her mother told her that the person who called was named Michelle and she gave Rachael the number to call in New York City. Rachael still thought she was being pranked. She called up the number ready to find out which of her friends was playing a joke on her. When a woman on the other end picked up and said, "Michelle of Today," Rachael was so stunned and scared that she hung up the phone immediately. It took here a minute to collect herself and realize this was the real deal. She called back and set the date to appear. Al Roker wanted her to show how to make four different hearty winter soups.

The snow did come as expected but that was not going to stop Ray. She packed her car with pots, pans, and food, and headed south. The story has gained embellishments as time has gone on but the drive took her around seven hours. The city, which she had sworn off, was now beckoning her back, and Rachael was ready for her triumphant return.

On the day of her appearance, March 6, 2001, Rachael was prepared. But it was no easy task. She had just over an hour to have all her soups ready for presentation. Moments of self-doubt were creeping up on her. She thought that she really was just a waitress from upstate New York—What was she doing here? But she didn't have too much time to question things. It helped that before she went on, host Katie Couric walked over to her, inhaled deep, and said, "That smells insanely good." Before she knew it, Roker was introducing the country to Rachael Ray, author of *Rachael Ray's 30-Minute Meals: Comfort Foods.* "You got very excited when I said that," Roker said. Ray replied, "Yeah, it's cool. Al's saying my name. Groovy." According to Ray, after the appearance people would stop her and tease her, saying, "Hey, Rachael! Groovy!"

She went on that day to tell Roker: "My grandfather is from Sicily, so for my mom a big pot of escarole and beans is comfort food. My dad's from down South, so for him, jambalaya is a comfort food. Me, I've always lived in the Northeast, so what we're going to make right now is comfort food for me."

She went on to show Roker how to make chicken and dumplings. Her performance was a home run. She was lively and fun and in her few minutes on air, she gave home viewers a great snapshot of who she was, where she was from, and what she was all about. The storm may have helped her too, because

Word of Ray's "30-minute" success upstate reached New York City. Soon, she was being booked on NBC's *Today Show*, showing weatherman Al Roker how to make soup. Although appearing on the show was nerve-wracking, Ray's personality and confidence shone through.

many more people were home from work that day, staying warm inside, and watching the television.

Things Start to Sizzle

While all this was going on, she had also gotten a call from the Food Network. It seemed that the old expression "When it rains, it pours" was coming true. The day after her *Today Show* appearance she was scheduled to meet with Food Network executives.

But Ray knew a lot about Food Network and she didn't see herself as in the same league as their chef heavy hitters. The Food Network was the home of Mario Batali, Emeril Lagasse, and Bobby Flay. These were chefs who owned and operated their own restaurants. Surely, she couldn't offer anything on their level.

So when Ray walked into the meeting with Food Network execs, she tried to set them straight right away: "I said, 'Listen, you're champagne, I'm beer out of the bottle,'" she said in *Vanity Fair* magazine. "'I clearly don't belong here, I'm not a chef, you've been duped.' And I got up. And they said, 'No, no, no, stop. That's what we like. We don't want you to be a chef.'"[3]

The Food Network bosses told her to sit down and relax. They told her she didn't need to be a full-fledged chef to have a hit show. They reminded her of Nigella Lawson, a British cooking celebrity who had written cookbooks but was not a trained chef. Also, at this stage in the Food Network history, the channel wasn't so sure that chefs were necessarily the answer to having high ratings. While *Iron Chef* featured real chefs, it was really the spectacle and crazy set-up of the show that drew in viewers. The traditional approach of having a chef simply demonstrate how to cook food seemed to be losing appeal.

What Does Rachael Ray Always Keep
★ in Her Kitchen

In her book *Rachael Ray Express Lane Meals: A 30-Minute Meal Cookbook* (Clarkson Potter, 2006), Rachael Ray revealed what she always keeps on hand in her kitchen. She always stocks extra virgin olive oil (which she calls EVOO), tomatoes, canned beans, cheese, and salami. Her book goes on to give a list of about seventy items, including spices for the spice rack, milk, butter, eggs, parmigiano-reggiano cheese, bacon, hot sauce, Dijon mustard, spicy brown mustard, capers, flat-leaf parsley, celery, carrots, mayonnaise.

In the freezer, she keeps on hand peas, corn, chopped spinach, and plain and Italian breadcrumbs. She also has Idaho potatoes, lemons, limes, onions, shallots, peanut butter, and garlic. In the cupboard, she keeps chicken stock, beef stock, diced tomatoes, crushed tomatoes, tomato paste, tomato sauce, chipotle chilies, black beans, long-cut pastas, short-cut pastas, couscous, white rice, all-purpose flour, white sugar, brown sugar, Italian tuna in EVOO, tuna in water, Alaskan salmon, Worcestershire sauce, vegetable oil, tamari, balsamic vinegar, red wine vinegar, honey, anchovies, roasted red peppers in water, and canned clams.

Bobby Flay is a highly-acclaimed chef with several top-tier restaurants to his name. But his transition to television personality was anything but smooth. In the beginning, the Food Network paired Flay with a co-host, Jacqui Malouf, who was tasked with getting the chef to articulate his process.

In addition, the roster of Food Network's celebrities needed some freshening. Emeril and Bobby Flay had been around for a while. They knew they had to keep fresh exciting talent coming down the TV pipeline.

Bob Tuschman was among those watching her cook with Al Roker the previous morning. On *Chefography*, Tuschman said that he thought her performance on the *Today Show* was astounding. She was fun and lit up the screen.

In the same *Vanity Fair* article, Brooke Johnson, president of the Food Network explained the power of Rachael: "Rachael came along with the right idea at the right time. Cooking used to be hours and hours in the kitchen, and obviously, with the number of workingwomen in this country, they don't have time to do it. Rachael figured that out and gave it a great name; really fun, interesting ingredients; ways to mix and match—just things you wouldn't think of."[4]

Plus, Johnson added that her big, big personality helped her. She said that Rachael isn't one to hide, and people like that. "She has tremendous energy," said Johnson. "She jumps off the screen."

> *"Rachael came along with the right idea at the right time. Cooking used to be hours and hours in the kitchen."*

Welcome to TV Land

The Food Network asked Ray to make a pilot and they teamed her up with Mark Dissin, who was known for his expertise in producing engaging television shows. At first, the two did not see eye to eye. Ray wanted to present recipes that featured an ingredient—so she might use her thirty minutes to present three dishes each with one distinctive ingredient. The idea may have been a holdover from Cowan & Lobel, where she used this approach to help sell products. Dissin, however, thought that the whole focus of the show should be about preparing a complete meal in thirty minutes—and the singular star ingredient for each dish should not be the focus. Dimmin's idea won out in the end.

Allen Salkin describes the first day of shooting of her pilot in his book *From Scratch*. Ray was not accustomed to filming a cable TV show, so it took her a little time to adjust. Dissin told her that when they began taping, she should not stop no matter what. This was a show about cooking in real time. She had to finish her 30-minute meal in thirty minutes and there could be no tricks. That made it different from some other shows where they could yell, "Stop camera!" and then pause and fix a recipe or recook something that wasn't going right.

Ray had a backup team off camera that was cooking a meal right along with her. Then if something did go wrong, they'd have a back up—if she burnt the vegetables, the backup team—in theory—could hand her the correct version of the dish. With the earphone on, she could also receive reminders and instructions from the director: "Stir the pasta." "Don't forget the nutmeg." "Add the salt." If she is missing a crucial step, it's helpful for Ray to have the reminder in her earphone.

Ray's nerves were somewhat rattled when she realized that they were filming on the same set where Emeril Lagasse shot his show. Every now and then his logo would be projected on the floor. She had to get used to wearing an earphone and taking instructions from the director through an earpiece. She would be told to look at camera one, turn to camera two, smile into camera three. This was a new ball game, and she had to learn fast. She asked the director that instead of referring to the cameras as numbers could he just yell out the cameraman's name instead. When the cameras started rolling, she told viewers that the show was all about preparing a meal from start to finish in just thirty minutes. Her opening two lines explaining the concept was all that was scripted. The rest was off the top of her head.

Although Rachael Ray's first on-camera demonstrations for Food Network executives were a little bumpy, she showed enough promise that they offered her a high-paying contract. Not only did Ray know how to teach people how to make easy meals, she could do it with lots of energy and a smile on her face. In fact, she made people want to cook.

Along the way in her demonstration, she had turned the burner on under a pan to preheat it. But she didn't pay too much attention to how hot it was getting. When it came time for her to pour about a tablespoon of olive oil into the skillet, the pan was now hot beyond expectation. She tilted the olive oil bottle and the second the oil hit the pan: FOOM! The oil instantly caught on fire and sent a four-foot flame shooting into the air. She jolted her head back in the nick of time so she didn't scorch her face. Before she could panic, she remembered her director's words—no matter what happened she was supposed to keep going. So, she kept her wits, and as calmly as she could, she grabbed some salt and threw it on the flame, putting out the fire quickly. She smoothly grabbed a cold pan, poured the oil in, and continued on with the show, smiling the entire time. The Food Network bosses liked what they saw. This woman radiated positive energy—even when she was almost burning down Emeril's set. And she was different from almost all their other culinary hosts. She wasn't a seasoned, trained professional chef—she was the hard-working common person who wanted to make a great meal fast for friends and family. She didn't speak like a highly trained chef, she spoke like an everyday person. The network ordered an initial batch of 25 episodes of *30 Minute Meals* and they'd see how it would go.

Ray also received the biggest payday of her life so far when the Food Network signed her to a $360,000 contract. The food buyer from upstate who was scraping by paycheck to paycheck could now breathe a little easier. According to an article in The *New York Times*, one of the first things she did was have all the furniture reupholstered in the upstate cabin. One of the next things she did was to buy the cabin.[5]

Chapter
5

America Discovers
Rachael Ray

The first episode of *30 Minute Meals* hit the airwaves on November 2, 2001. Again, it wasn't accident-free. During one of her stories, she took her Santoku knife (a general-use Japanese kitchen knife) and nearly cut her finger off. She says that staff literally glued it back on using Krazy Glue, and they kept taping, with Rachael smiling all the way. On the website sheknows.com, Rachael said, "Now that finger is like a trick finger and at parties I can stick it in an open flame and make money on how long I can leave it there because I can't really feel anything," she said. "Yeah, it never fell off but it's pretty dead."[1]

In her first few episodes, it was obvious that Ray was trying to find her way and get comfortable. She was a little more shy and quiet than the Rachael that many knew. But she was a fast learner and she soon was going full-tilt, not holding back on being herself.

During these early days as she shot her first episodes, the Food Network called on Bobby Flay to get his opinion of her.

Fellow Food Network Star
Bobby Flay gave Rachael
his official endorsement.
She had the one thing he
didn't when he started out:
She was a natural in front
of the camera.

He watched her for twenty minutes and he knew in that short amount of time that she had something special. She had that special ingredient: She was good at being herself in front of the camera. She was natural. When Flay came over to talk to her, she was stunned again. She couldn't get over that real celebrity chefs were treating her seriously. "You're not trying to be anybody else," Flay said in the book *From Scratch*. "People will relate to you immediately."[2]

> *"You're not trying to be anybody else. People will relate to you immediately."*
>
> *—Chef Bobby Flay in the book* From Scratch.

Emeril Lagasse, on the other hand, didn't immediately like Rachael. He liked the idea of seeing real chefs on the Food Network. He thought she was an amateur and would ultimately hurt the channel. In time, however, even he was won over by the positive and perky Rachael. Other people on staff reportedly felt the same as Lagasse—they thought working behind the scenes they knew much more about cooking for a TV show than Ray.

But Ray was also the right person at the right time. Her show was airing just a few months after the terrorist attacks on the World Trade Center and elsewhere in the U.S. on September 11, 2001. The American public was looking for comfort and returning to old-fashioned values. They were thinking of their home and spending time with their families, doing things like cooking homemade meals.

Ray's show was a hit. She was helping people reconnect with their kitchens. In a strange twist, the attacks had given the Food Network a lift in ratings. Ratings were about 25 percent

Emeril Lagasse bristled at the idea of including cooks, rather than chefs, on the Food Network. Lagasse believed the hosts should have more extensive credentials than Ray had. However, Lagasse quickly came around once he got to know Ray and understand her methods.

higher in 2001 compared to 2000, and during that time period the Food Network expanded its reach into millions more homes.

Also, Ray was not dressed like a professional chef. She was wearing her everyday clothes—just like the audience she appealed to. And when she went to get her ingredients from the fridge, they weren't all pre-chopped and ready to go. She walked to the refrigerator, filled her arms with what she needed, and walked back to the counter. Sometimes, she just made it to the counter without dropping everything on the floor. That trip to the fridge seemed like a simple thing—but it was a big difference from how the other chefs were demonstrating cooking. This was how real people had to prepare a meal, so this was how she was going to do it. There was no "food stylist" on set who was perfectly browning turkey skin or making the ideal crisp on the top of a pie. What you saw was what you got. And this no-gimmicks approach struck a chord with the viewing public.

She was showing TV viewers how to make smothered kale and mushrooms, parmesan-herb chicken tenders, thin crust pizza, veggie and penne with pesto, spicy shrimp aglio e olio, Brooklyn Barbecue chili burgers, salmon sweet potato cakes, and Spanish chicken and dumplings. She was creating dishes that people could make with ingredients found in grocery stores, like the ones in her hometown. She used lots of olive oil, but steered clear of truffle oil. She uses boxed ingredients like corn muffin mix to make her Cracked Corn and Cheese Squares. She'd be flipping burgers, not sautéing veal cheeks. She made "Super Sloppy Joes," not Beef Wellington. Her recipes include "Dilly of a Quesadilla," "Cashew! God Bless You Chicken," and "You Won't Be Single for Long Vodka and Cream Pasta." She was showing the masses how to make her version of jambalaya,

Food Network audiences found Ray appealing precisely because she was not like the hosts of other cooking shows. She was a regular person cooking recipes that could be followed and made by the average cook.

which she says is "like jambalaya" so naturally she calls it "jambalika."

Some in the cooking world complained that many of her recipes were just too simple. In The *New York Times*, for example, William Grimes asked the question, do you really need a recipe to explain how to make prosciutto (pro-shoot-o) and melon?[3] One of her dessert recipes for Black Cherry Ice Cream with Chocolate Sauce was simply to pour chocolate sauce over the ice cream. Others criticized her for using so many packaged products. Jill Pellettieri, a reporter and a huge fan of Ray's, wrote about her experience trying the 30-minute recipes in *Slate*.[4] Pellettieri could not complete one in thirty minutes. While some loved Ray's personality, others said she giggled and talked too much. And although she embraced making mistakes and not using measurements, others wanted a more accurate approach.

A Style All Her Own

Still, huge audiences were embracing her style—she was down-to-earth, the friendly neighbor. She was attractive but not threatening. She showed a people that cooking could be fun and uncomplicated. She took the stuffiness out of cooking. Some people who watched highly trained chefs on TV thought they could never cook like that. But then here's Ray—your ordinary person with no official culinary training—and people are thinking, if she can do it, so can I. Some thought of her as the anti-Martha Stewart. Martha Stewart had built an empire showing people how to do things properly and accurately. But Rachael was all about not following the rules, making some mistakes and having fun. Her strong work ethic made it easy for

Rachael Ray's TV show brought in big ratings for the network. She published more cookbooks under their banner and soon became one of the most recognizable faces of the Food Network.

her to shoot three shows a day, and for Rachael talking while cooking was effortless.

You can tell she doesn't necessarily like rules from the way she handles her measurements. She usually steers clear of teaspoons, tablespoons and other official measurements. She prefers a pinch of this, a couple glugs of that, a handful or palmful here, and a shake over there.

Just like Emeril had his expressions "BAM!" and "Let's kick it up a notch," Rachael had her phrases and unique terms. She

Rachael Ray captivated audiences with her easy smile and outgoing personality, simple but creative recipes, and her energetic, fun way of talking. Soon, viewers were pouring "EVOO" into their skillets and throwing foodscraps into a "garbage bowl."

would often say "How cool is that?" "Let her rip!" and "Yum-o!" She'd often use non-culinary terms like screamin' hot, smokin' and shimmy shake. She also coined many other cooking phrases. Ray's *30 Minute Meals* became the Food Network's highest-rated show.

Others saw the popularity of Ray's 30-minute approach and tried to jump on the bandwagon. The *For Dummies* series of books put out *30-Minute Meals for Dummies*. Even the highly praised and respected Jacques Pepin wanted to show home audiences how to cook delicious food fast so he started a PBS series called *Fast Food My Way*. Eventually, the young English chef Jamie Oliver would top Ray's 30-minute meals with his book *15-Minute Meals*. (If you scour the Internet, you'll even find some five-minute meals out there.) Ray topped herself in fact: In her book *Just in Time*, she presents a group of 15-minute meals as well.

Rachael Ray's
★ Turns of Phrase

Ray has developed her own way of describing food. Here is a short guide to some of her popular expressions and terms.

Canoodle It: Speed it up and simplify it

GH: a grownup helper when the kitchen has child chefs at work

Sammies: Sandwiches

Stoups: Soups that are thick like stews

Two turns of the pan: Enough olive oil to cover the bottom of a pan it two turns—about two tablespoons (30 mL)

EVOO: Extra virgin olive oil (Ray has said that it takes too long to say extra virgin olive oil.) The phrase became so widely used that in 2007 the *Oxford American College Dictionary* included it as an official word

Yum-o: Yummy

De-lish: Delicious

Easy-peasy: Very easy

Garbage Bowl or GB: A bowl used while cooking

Chapter
6

Making Time for
a Personal Life

Just as things were taking off with *30 Minute Meals*, Ray was about to have some more success on a personal level. In 2001, Rachael attended a birthday party filled with glamorous—and tall—actors and models. Across the room, she spied someone who was attractive and more her own height. The man was John Cusimano. He stood five foot seven—just about three inches taller than Rachael. (Cusimano said that they saw each other in "a sea of knees.") Cusimano was an entertainment lawyer and the lead singer in a band called The Cringe. Like Rachael, he was Italian-American and he loved to cook. In *People* magazine, she said that she saw John from across the room immediately. "I couldn't take my eyes off him. I was speechless and I'm never speechless."[1]

Somehow, she managed to talk. She introduced herself and said she was a host on a Food Network show. He had never seen her, but he told her that he loved food. According to *People* magazine's blog, Ray asked what types of foods he cooked. She thought he'd say something basic like chili or chicken Parmesan.

He told her that the night before the party he had made a tilapia with a tomatillo-jalapeño-cilantro reduction with a little bit of Negro Modelo beer and a maque choux (mock-choo) on the side. Rachael thought this guy couldn't be real. She said to him, "Alright, I'm going to be eating some of that food." [2]

She related to the fact that Cusimano was Italian as well. "I'm only Italian from the stomach down — John's one hundred percent!" Ray says they have been together ever since that night. "We've been plastered on each other, making people sick ever since then," she said on *Larry King Live*. [3] She added in *People* that "He came at a point in my life when I had decided, I'm not going to chase [marriage]. I don't think young men or women should feel pressured into marriage. You shouldn't marry anyone, in my opinion, who you have to try hard for." [4]

> *"You shouldn't marry anyone, in my opinion, who you have to try hard for."*

The two have had a cozy relationship. They have dinner almost every night—even if that meal has to be at midnight because of Ray's long days. Cusimano often does the dishes after his wife cooks. He loves her cooking. On one of his birthdays, she offered to make him any dish he would like— lobster, steak, fish. But Cusimano just wanted one of Ray's family favorites: Carbonara. For Rachael, that was just another sign that they were meant to be together. The one food area where he is in charge is the coffee because Ray says that is one thing she cannot make. "My coffee either looks like cat pee or mud and it tastes worse than either," she said on *Larry King Live*. [5]

Rachael met entertainment lawyer John Cusimano at a party. The fellow Italian American shared her love of food. Cusimano has helped Ray take her business to the next level.

In the documentary series *Biography*, Cusimano said that they have a great relationship because Ray is his "buddy." "She's the person I want to talk to about everything. Nothing really seems real until she knows about it and vice versa. If you are living with your best friend, life is great."

A Boyfriend Grows a Brand

Their relationship grew especially close because Cusimano became part of Ray's professional world as well. Early on in their relationship, Rachael sat down with Cusimano and told him how fans were writing to her or coming to her at book signings and asking how they could buy Rachael Ray products. At this stage, she had no items with her name on them. In *From Scratch*, Allen Salkin describes how Ray always kept a garbage bowl on her cooking counter so she could easily get rid of her food scraps and mess as she cooked. This was the type of item fans might want to buy. Or they might go for a knife like the special Japanese style one she used. Or she had a hybrid mop/towel that she used to handle hot items and wipe or dry kitchen cookware. She called it a "moppine." Ray also showed Cusimano her idea for a spaghetti pot. Thin dry spaghetti didn't fit easily in a standard pot. A home chef has to get one end of the noodles cooking and then slowly ease in the portion of the noodles that are still sticking above water level. Rachael's spaghetti pot was thinner and longer and the spaghetti would go right in. The pot was also compact—ideal for small apartments.

As an entertainment lawyer, John had been spending a lot of his time marketing small independent films. Now, he hitched his career to Ray's. He agreed to help get deals to make Rachael Ray products. Within a short time, he struck deals with various cookware companies to produce a Rachael Ray line of garbage

Rachael Ray—
Music Fan

Ray loves to listen to music while she cooks and her tastes are wide-ranging. She enjoys rock from Foo Fighters, U2, and Muse. She likes her husband's band, The Cringe. Some favorite songs are "Train in Vain," by The Clash; "Brass in Pocket," by The Pretenders;

Cusimano has a band on the side, and Ray loves to join in. She is a big music fan and has a huge record collection.

"Landslide," by Fleetwood Mac; Elvis Costello's "(What's So Funny 'Bout) Peace, Love & Understanding?"; and U2's "Where the Streets Have No Name." She also loves jazz—Louis Armstrong, Keely Smith, and Chet Baker. Even opera gets played in her kitchen. Luciano Pavarotti is a favorite. Since 2008, she has hosted the "Feedback Party" at the music festival South by Southwest in Austin, Texas. She's hosted some bands there that have gone on to become more famous, such as Imagine Dragons, The Civil Wars, and Edward Sharpe and the Magnetic Zeros. "Music feeds your soul," Rachael said in *ET Online*. "It makes everyone come out in one way or another and just get freaky with it." On *MTV News*, she said, "People think I'm like this food robot or something, but music is a huge part of my life." She has a vinyl collection of 1,500 to 2,000 records. She says that she developed a love of jazz and opera through her father.

bowls, knives, and oval spaghetti pots. In time, her cookware line would grow to include a wide range of pots, pans, utensils, "moppines," and more. She would eventually expand to sheets and blankets with her name on them. Her products would be sold in major department stores, including Target and Macy's, where she had gotten her start.

Ray would also go on to endorse products that she likes and uses—like Ziploc bags, Nabisco products, and Dunkin' Donuts. She was criticized for the Dunkin' Donuts endorsement because she has been such an advocate for teaching kids how to eat healthy. Donuts aren't exactly a nutrtious treat. She has also come out with her own line of ingredients that she often uses—EVOO, balsamic vinegar, chicken stock, and beef stock. She would also go on in 2007 to sign a deal with AT&T to provide "Recipes on the Run" to wireless subscribers. Within a few years, Rachael Ray would become a multi-million dollar business.

Wedding Bells

After being together about four years, Cusimano proposed to Ray. She went crazy when he popped the question, screaming with joy and punching him in disbelief. On September 24, 2005, the couple got married in a castle in the Tuscany region of Italy. They chose the town of Montalcino because their favorite wine, Brunello, came from that area. Many of Ray's old friends and family were there, including her publisher Hiroko Kiiffner, her sister, and her mother. After the wedding, the couple took off for a honeymoon in Africa. Her mother Elsa loved Tuscany as well and she brought the feel of Tuscany to the beloved Ray cabin in the Adirondacks—the garden, the stone paths, fire pits, benches, and bocce court are all reminders of Italy.

With Cusimano's help, Ray began selling food products and cookware bearing her name, as well as endorsing products she loves and uses.

The Animal Lover

Cusimano and Ray have not planned to have children. Ray has said that she loves hanging out with children and cooking with them, but he has honestly felt that she did not have time to raise them. She dedicates an enormous amount of time to her work and she likes her life that way. Although she does not have children, she has always been a dog lover and tended well to her dogs. She has said that her dog is her child. For a long time—twelve years—she had a pit bull named Boo. When Boo got older, Rachael cooked her pooch a special barley and brown rice mix that she called Boosotto.

Rachael Ray is an unabashed dog lover. She developed her own line of healthy, natural dog food called Nutrish. All of Nutrish's proceeds go toward animal rescue.

In 2005, the year she was happily married, her beloved Boo died suddenly. Ray was absolutely devastated and didn't sleep for days. She had an idea that maybe Boo's spirit could have transferred to another pit bull. She said she searched 2,000 rescue sites and pit bull sites for a little puppy that reminded her of Boo. Finally, she found a newborn pup with a little dot in the middle of its forehead. She thought that this was a sign. She got the pup and named her Isaboo.[6]

It's probably no surprise that after cooking for her dogs and developing her own pet food recipes, Ray got into the pet food biz as well. She has a natural pet food line for dogs and cats called Nutrish, and all proceeds go to her charity to rescue at-risk animals. As of 2015, her mother kept 15 rescue cats.

Chapter
7

An Expanding
Empire

With the unexpected success of *30 Minute Meals*, the Food Network thought it should take advantage of Ray's soaring popularity. On *Larry King Live*, Ray explained that she heard that the network was considering doing as show based on the concept of "Rich Man, Poor Man." One guy would get $500 and another would get $50 and they'd compare what they did with the money. Ray had already done a budget travel show upstate, so she told the TV executives that she thought a straight-up budget travel show would be better because everybody—rich or poor—likes to save money. They agreed for her to film a show about eating and traveling in the U.S. called *$40 a Day*. Ray would offer tips on what to see in different cities, as well as advice on how to save and find bargains in these areas. The program began airing in April 2002, just five months after *30 Minute Meals* had made its debut.

As this show grew in popularity, Ray expanded her travels to Canada and Europe as well. She went to Los Angeles, Miami, Seattle, San Francisco, Portland, Las Vegas, Charlestown,

Expanding on the success of *30 Minute Meals*, the Food Network approved Ray's idea for a second show. In 2000, she debuted *$40 a Day*, a travel show that had Ray on a food budget of $40. Ray enjoyed traveling, meeting new people, and of course, trying new foods.

Washington, DC, Rome, Paris, Brussels, Florence, and Tuscany, to name a few locations. On the program, she shows how to dine everywhere from crab shacks to brew pubs to five-star restaurants. One of her rules was to avoid all fast food restaurants. In Rome, she enjoyed spaghetti alla carbonara, antipasti, magro di Maile alla Mazio (marinated pork), and gelato ice cream. In Boston, she had a great breakfast from a local farmer's market and an amazing seafood lunch.

The show was popular but ended in 2005 when Ray basically updated the concept and began a program called *Rachael Ray's Tasty Travels*. With Rachael fever still running high, this show debuted with the second highest ratings in Food Network history. Only *Iron Chef America* had higher ratings for its first episode. In *Rachael Ray's Tasty Travels*, Ray visited different cities, often traveling with her husband, and highlighted her favorite places, including those that were more on the pricey side. However, she still made sure to give her "Hot List of Values" because she knew many people tuned her in to see where to eat on a budget. Even if she visited a fancy restaurant, she gave tips on the best bargains at those eateries. On her visit to Baltimore, she visited Faidley Seafood, which has been making crab cakes since 1886. They also sell something that can only be found in Baltimore—the coddy—a mixture of salt crackers, mustard and codfish fried up. Ray also introduced viewers to the old-style diner Café Hon, where the owner sports a beehive hairdo and a diner can get a meatloaf dinner for under $12.

The year 2005 turned out to be an especially good one for Ray. With four hot programs in rotation at the Food Network, she was attracting upward of 18 million viewers per week. Because she also started a magazine called *Every Day with Rachael Ray*, she was wearing a new hat. She was editor-in-chief

One episode of Ray's next show, *Rachael Ray's Tasty Travels*, brought her to a replica of the Oval Office at the Clinton Presidential Library & Museum in Little Rock, Arkansas. Years later, Ray would be a guest at the real White House.

After she had proven herself to be a successful television personality, Rachael Ray turned to magazines. *Every Day with Rachael Ray* is a food and lifestyle magazine launched in 2005 that is still going strong.

of her own lifestyle magazine. The magazine business is notoriously difficult. Many publications fail. But Ray seemed to be on an amazing roll. She struck a deal with Reader's Digest.

By 2006, the magazine, with its motto of "Take a bite out of life," was heading toward a circulation of 1.7 million. The philosophy behind the magazine was the same as behind many of her shows. You don't have to be rich to have a rich life. So her magazine is filled with tips to help people live better lives on the cheap. When the first issue came out, Reader's Digest did a print run of 300,000. But as might be expected, it sold out fast. Reader's Digest returned to the presses three times to keep up with demand for that first issue and eventually it sold more than one million copies. The magazine has remained a popular publication and the Meredith Corporation purchased it from Reader's Digest in 2011.

Rachael Ray's philosophy: You don't have to be rich to have a rich life.

Along the way, in 2004, Ray began creating yet another show called *Inside Dish*. This was a hybrid of cooking show and a talk show celebrities dropping by to pay a visit. In some ways, this show is a precursor of the hit syndicated talk show she would later develop. The guests included Ryan Seacrest, Tony Danza, Dennis Franz, and Gloria Estefan. She visited the actor Morgan Freeman at his Ground Zero juke joint in Clarksdale, Mississippi, and got him out on the dance floor. With Gloria Estefan, she found out what she had in her refrigerator at home. She got the answer to big celebrity food questions such as Where does Mekhi Phifer chow down after a long day on the *ER* set? What special diet keeps Mariel

Hemingway glowing and healthy? What's the secret to Dennis Franz's crab cakes?

While the professional cooking world had been dominated by male chefs, Ray seemed to be part of a new movement in the early 2000s. Now, women in food appeared to be taking over and getting the spotlight. On the Food Network, the female stars were getting all the attention. Besides Rachael Ray, women cooks like Giada De Laurentiis, Paula Deen, Sandra Lee, Ina Garten, and Nigella Lawson were attracting big audiences. As a young attractive female, Ray was gaining a lot of male viewers as well.

In 2003, she was approached by FHM (For Him Magazine) to do a photo shoot. Ray thought at first that FHM meant Food and Home. Although her mother was furious with her decision, Rachael decided to go ahead and do a "sexy" but tasteful photo shoot for the magazine. She had always thought that she looked a little "Frodo-like," so it was a boost for her ego to be considered sexy. Naturally, her appearance in the magazine gained her tons of publicity, and she noticed that more young males were showing up at book signings, so her audience grew even bigger.

Becoming a Chef

For many, the path to becoming a cook or chef is similar to Rachael Ray's in that you have to learn the skills by doing. She worked long hours in many restaurants and food shops to learn the food business, and then she cooked, cooked, cooked. Work experience is the main ingredient to landing many chef jobs. Many top chefs like Emeril Lagasse, Anthony Bourdain, Michael Mina, Grant Achatz, David Chang, and Todd English all went to culinary school. Mario Batali attended London's Cordon Bleu for a short time but dropped out, deciding he would learn more

While many chefs earned degrees from culinary institutes, others, like Rachael, have learned through life experience. Ina Garten, the Barefoot Contessa, was a White House nuclear energy budget analyst who liked to cook. She learned from cookbooks and by hosting dinner parties.

from great chefs who were working at top restaurants. Pro chefs Ashley Christensen, Barbara Lynch, and Susan Goin did not go to culinary school. By just learning on the job, they paved their way to success.

While culinary school isn't necessary, it can provide a want-to-be chef with the skills needed to enter a kitchen and perform from the get-go. Even knowing the language of cooking (names of sauces, methods of heating, etc.) can go a long way when entering a professional kitchen. Most programs cover all the bases when it comes to working in a restaurant. Beyond cooking techniques (like knife skills) and kitchen operations, culinary school courses cover menu planning, food sanitation procedures, and purchasing and inventory methods. Most training programs also require students to get real-world experience. Through connections from their schools, students may complete internships or apprenticeships in commercial kitchens. Some community colleges and technical schools also offer professional training in cooking. More than 200 academic training programs at post-secondary schools are accredited through the American Culinary Federation (ACF). The ACF also organizes certification programs—chefs that receive certification demonstrate that they have reached a certain level of competence. Students should keep in mind that cooking school can be expensive and may require paying back loans for years to come.

The Bureau of Labor Statistics lists the following talents as being important to succeeding at job:

Business skills. Many chefs run their own business or are in charge of the finances at a restaurant. They can benefit from learning how to handle administrative tasks, such as accounting and personnel management, and be able to manage a restaurant efficiently and profitably.

Communication skills. Chefs need to be able to communicate quickly and clearly with their staff to make sure food is being executed properly and brought to the tables in an efficient manner.

Creativity. The chefs who truly shine come up with their own dishes. They take time to be creative and develop interesting and innovative recipes. They should be able to use various ingredients to create appealing meals for their customers.

Dexterity. For chefs and head cooks, their job depends on fast, clean and precise cutting techniques. It's all in the hands—so manual dexterity is a must.

Leadership skills. Chefs need to motivate, instruct, and organize kitchen staff to get meals completed and served. Developing a cooperative atmosphere of staff is an essential skill.

Chapter

8

The Oprah of
Cooking

Rachael had once told her mom that one of her dreams was to be on Oprah Winfrey's talk show. In keeping with the rest of her life, which was all about making dreams come true, this one would soon be realized. When her Food Network shows took off and her popularity soared, Oprah invited Ray to be on her show. On *Larry King Live*, Ray recalled that the first time Oprah's team called for her to be on the show. She was on book tour and the planes were delayed. She was scrambling to get to Oprah's studio and "on the verge of tears."

"I was such a basket case," she told King. "I thought I was terrible and nervous and too bobble head-like for Oprah and the likes of her show. And when we went to break, she leaned in and said, 'Hey, you're terrific. Keep on being you.' And I thought, oh my gosh, that's Oprah talking to me!"[1]

When Ray appeared on *Oprah* in 2005, the famous talk show host told her that the reason for Ray's success was her great personality and her accessibility. She called Rachael Ray a super cook and the queen of quick and easy. Ray appeared on the show many times after her first visit.

Oprah saw great potential in a Rachael Ray talk show that also centered around food. King World (a TV production company) and Oprah's company Harpo thought Ray would be great on daytime TV and they teamed up to make a talk show. After a deal was hammered out, Ray got to work planning the show. They reportedly shot five pilots before settling on the final format.

The basic concept was for Ray to bring various celebrities onto the program to discuss their accomplishments in entertainment, sports, or other media. Ray might present tips and strategies for staying healthy and safe from various health and lifestyle experts. She would also include makeover segments,

Successful appearances on *The Oprah Winfrey Show* led Winfrey to offer Ray her own daytime show. The Winfrey-produced syndicated talk show *Rachael Ray* premiered in 2006.

and possibly musical performances. At some point, her guest would join her to cook up some food in her TV kitchen. The motto of her show is don't just talk—taste, touch, do, and the show follows a mission to help people find simple solutions to everyday problems.

The biggest obstacle for Ray to get over was talking to a live audience. Her shows on the Food Network were either filmed on location or in a studio without an audience. Still, Rachael was comfortable talking with people on book tours and from her days doing live demos at Price Chopper. She told the studio audience about her nervousness on the first show, explaining that for five years she was on the Food Network "talking to vegetables." Also, on the first show, Rachael injured herself. She seemed to have knack for having small accidents on her first shows. This time she was moving her hands with nervous energy, and she cut her cuticle on a whisk.

In the fall of 2006, her daytime syndicated talk show turned into another blockbuster hit. The program averaged about 2.6 million viewers daily at the start and now attracts about 1.7 million viewers. Oprah has been a guest on her show, stopping in to make pizza one episode. Diane Sawyer threw apples at the audience. And a cavalcade of celebrities was to follow. Ray says that her secret to interviewing is realizing that these stars are just people, too. And she asks them unusual questions: If you were a superhero, what would your power be? What's your secret talent? She makes sure to have an actual conversation with all who visit her.

She also does great things for her viewers. In 2015, Ray offered a tuition competition with a grand prize worth $41,500. It includes free tuition for either a six-month day or nine-month night Professional Culinary Arts Program at the International

Hosting her daytime talk show has allowed Ray to expand her talents. Segments on the show have her interviewing celebrities, cooking, talking to audience members, discussing beauty and style, and offering home design tips, among other things.

Ray has hosted a wide range of guests on her talk show, from legendary singer Tony Bennett to the Kardashians. In 2012, First Lady Michelle Obama stopped by to play a game called "Pop the Question."

Culinary Center in New York City, as well as a five-night culinary vacation at Finest Playa Mujeres Resort in Cancun, Mexico. She has awarded families new kitchens and she granted a young girl with a heart defect her Make-a-Wish wish of cooking with her on her program.

Time magazine declared that the perky girl next door who now headed a media empire had made their list of top 100 men and women whose power, talent or moral example is transforming our world in 2006. The show went on to win two Emmy awards for Outstanding Talk Show in 2008 and 2009. In 2015, the show was entering its 10th season.

Staying Herself Even When Famous

Ray has admitted that she might not be the most slender or fit but that's because she wants to enjoy her food and wine. In *Good Housekeeping*, she explained that she just doesn't care that much about putting on a few extra pounds. She said she doesn't want to sacrifice wine and food to fit in a smaller size dress. And she's not a big gym buff either. She promises herself to go regularly, but she winds up going once a month. In many ways, her audience members can relate to this and they love her all the more. When Ray was on the *Larry King Show*, one caller said that she and her husband love to watch her and "we're glad you're not a twig."[2]

Typically taping about 285 shows a year between her Food Network shows and her talk show, Rachael has become busier than ever. Still, even with an over-packed schedule, what does she like to do most to relax at the end of a busy day? Cook! In *Chefography*, her husband said that after cooking all day, Rachael likes nothing better than coming home and cooking for the two of them. She doesn't crave going out to fancy restaurants or heading to celebrity parties. What she wants most is to be home with her dog, preparing a meal for her husband. "I'm the luckiest stomach on the planet," said John Cusimano.

Cusimano wrote in the foreword to *Rachael Ray's Book of 10*: "She avoids the label 'chef' and she feels she's not worthy since she's not had the formal training required and subsequent diploma or 'papers' as she calls them. She truly finds joy in cooking. Even after a long day at work, during which she would have cooked at least three to six full meals on camera, she can't wait to get home to unwind by—you guessed it—cooking. And drinking (typically an Italian red). And living, savoring, and slurping up every little nuance and big event in the lives of her friends and family."[3]

Occasionally, Rachael does like to spike these quiet times with some adventures—one of her favorites activities is skydiving!

Earning Millions and Giving Back

By 2009, Rachael was now earning $18 million a year, according to *ABC News*. In 2015, the website TheRichest.com reported that Rachael Ray was worth $60 million. "It makes me a little sick," she said on ABC News. "It makes my stomach flip. I'm not comfortable with it ... because I don't like to think of my life as that far away from me. People that make that kind of money—it's just too foreign of an idea."[5]

Knowing she now had more money than she personally would ever need, Ray wanted to give back to the world. In 2007, she put together the Yum-o! Organization. Although she decided not to have kids of her own, she loves kids and this is a way to help many of them. The mission of her nonprofit group was to help children eat healthier, more nutritious meals at home and at school. The organization teaches families to cook, feeds hungry kids, and funds cooking education and scholarships. *Rachael Ray Yum-O! The Family Cookbook* is filled with recipes that fulfill her organization's mission. Many recipes have been submitted to Ray from real families. In her book, she says that the mission of Yum-O! is to empower kids and their families to develop healthy relationships with food and cooking.

"We want to see a country where everyone can experience the joys of food and cooking," she writes in the introduction.[6] On the yum-o.org website there are more recipes for kids of

Top Three Pieces of
★ Career Advice

In *Forbes* magazine, Rachael offered these tips for living:

1. Take your work very seriously, but don't take yourself too seriously.

2. Work harder than the next person, and don't complain about it.

3. It's important that you understand that goals should never be money, or fame, or a television show. A goal has to be something that's more about your message as a contributor. What are you offering people with your job? That's a tough thing for people to understand sometimes. People make decisions just based on who's going to pay them the most, and I don't think that's a good strategy for life. You have to do what makes you happy and something that involves some larger purpose or message. I think that work that's done just to be work is meaningless.[4]

Rachael Ray is on a mission to get kids to adopt healthful lifestyles. Here, she visits an elementary school to promote healthy eating.

every age and skill level. There are stories from kids who love to cook. If you want to get involved and help in your community, there is a section "How Cool Is That?" Organizations are listed here that are making a difference in the world. The book includes recipes such as one-pot cacciatore stoup, My Mom's baked apples (a favorite from when Rachael was growing up), tortilla scrambles, and peanut butter and jelly French Toast. The organization has a Healthy, Hunger-Free Kids Act program that lobbies for related laws. Yum-o! projects also reach schools all over the country, getting healthier food to students and lowering the obesity rates.

Even More TV

When the Cooking Channel came along, Rachael Ray began shooting a new program in 2010 called *Week in a Day*. On this show, she prepares five meals for the week ahead in one day. The idea behind this program is to have great food ready ahead of time for the workweek when most people don't have the time or energy to cook.

In 2012, she appeared on *Rachael vs. Guy*. On this show, she and Food Network host Guy Fieri work with teams of celebrities in cooking competition. Rachael loves games, but this was an intense competition show that she just barely squeezed into

Ray worked with teenage chefs on a benefit dinner in honor of her Yum-o charity. Yum-o provides scholarships to budding chefs, helps families in need, and promotes healthy lifestyles for children.

her busy schedule. Olympians, actors, rap singers competed but none were professional cooks. Filming required twelve-to-fourteen hour days. Rachael and Guy coached their teams but they couldn't touch the food and physically help. She was impressed with how these non-chefs performed under pressure—cooking for a high number of people or for a world-class chef. Rachael and Guy also have *Rachael vs. Guy Kids Cook-Off* in which kids compete in cooking challenges. She has also found time to direct some contestants on *The Next Food Network Star*, coaching them on how to behave and perform on camera.

> *"Having self-worth, no matter what's your job is what matters, and being able to provide for yourself matters."*

If you want to keep up with what Rachael Ray is doing today, you have follow her on Twitter and Facebook. It seems certain, that she will have many new projects in the works if you check her updates.

In *Forbes*, Ray said, "Having self-worth, no matter what's your job is what matters, and being able to provide for yourself matters. These are things that matter; cash doesn't matter. Success will come and go, but finding that pride at the end of the day that you did your best job, and being able to cook for yourself and for the people you love. When I look back over my life, those are the most important things that I find."[7]

Try It Yourself!

Roasted Chickpeas
Serves 6

Ingredients

3 cans chickpeas

4 tablespoons (15mL) olive oil

3 tablespoons lemon juice

1/2-1 teaspoon each of your choice of spices, such as cumin, chili powder, cayenne pepper, curry, turmeric, and/or ginger

1 teaspoon garlic powder

1 teaspoon paprika

Salt and pepper, to taste

Directions

1.) Pre-heat the oven to 400°F. (205°C)

2.) Using a colander, drain and rinse chickpeas.

3.) Lay them out flat on paper towels to dry.

4.) Meanwhile, line a baking sheet with foil or parchment paper and spray with nonstick cooking spray.

5.) Combine the olive oil, lemon juice, and spices in a small bowl and whisk to combine.

6.) Move the chick peas to the cookie sheet.

7.) Pour the mixture over the chickpeas and toss until evenly coated. Make sure to lay chickpeas flat on the cookie sheet for even cooking.

8.) Season with salt and pepper.

9.) Bake for thirty-five to forty-five minutes, until browned and crispy. Serve hot or at room temperature.

Spaghetti Carbonara

Serves 4

Ingredients

8 ounces (240 mL) spaghetti

2 large eggs

1 cup (180 mL) grated Parmesan

4 slices bacon or pancetta, diced

4 cloves garlic, minced

Kosher salt and black pepper, to taste

1 cup frozen green peas

2 tablespoons (30 mL) chopped fresh
   parsley leaves

Directions

1.) In a large pot of boiling salted water, cook pasta according to package instructions. Add green peas. Drain well and reserve 1/2 cup (120mL) water.

2.) In a small bowl, whisk together eggs and Parmesan.

3.) Heat a large skillet over medium high heat. Add bacon and cook until brown and crispy, about 6-8 minutes. Reserve the cooking fat.

4.) Stir garlic into bacon fat, cooking until you can smell it (about 1 minute). Reduce heat to low.

5.) Quickly stir in pasta, then egg mixture. Gently fold with tongs to combine. Season with salt and pepper according to your tastes.

6.) Add reserved pasta water, one tablespoon at a time, until a creamy sauce forms, coating the pasta.

7.) Garnish with fresh parsley and serve.

Brownies à la Mode

Serves 6

Ingredients

1 stick (8 tablespoons) (60g) butter

2 squares unsweetened chocolate

1 cup (200g) sugar

2 eggs

1/2 teaspoon vanilla

1/4 cup (120 mL) all-purpose flour

1/4 teaspoon salt

1 cup (240mL) chopped walnuts (optional)

1/2 cup vanilla ice cream (per brownie)

Directions

1.) Spread butter along bottom and sides of an 8x8-inch (20x20 cm) square pan. Shake a tablespoon of flour along inside, until well coated.

2.) Melt 1 stick butter and 2 squares unsweetened chocolate. Remove the saucepan from heat, so ingredients don't burn.

3.) Stir in 1 cup sugar. Add 2 eggs and 1/2 teaspoon vanilla, and beat the mixture well.

4.) Stir in 1/4 cup all-purpose flour and 1/4 teaspoon salt. (In the original recipe, 1 cup chopped walnuts is added here as well.)

5.) Bake the brownies at 325°F (163°C) for about forty minutes, or until a toothpick can be removed cleanly from the batter.

6.) Let brownies cool before cutting into squares and topping with vanilla ice cream.

Puttanesca Pasta

Serves 4

Ingredients

---

8 ounces or 1/2 lb (230g) whole-wheat thin spaghetti, vermicelli, or angel hair

1 tablespoon extra-virgin olive oil

2 cloves garlic, minced

1/3 cup (80mL) chopped flat-leaf parsley

1/4 cup (60 mL) pitted and chopped green olives

2 tablespoons capers

1 teaspoon anchovy paste

1 tablespoon capers

1 tablespoon fresh (or 1 tsp dried) oregano leaves

1/8 teaspoon crushed red pepper flakes

1 14-ounce (400g) can low sodium diced tomatoes

3/4 cup (180mL) chopped fresh arugula

1/4 cup(120 mL) grated Parmesan

Directions

1.) Boil water in a large pot. Add pasta and cook according to the directions on the package (usually about seven minutes for *al dente*).

2.) While the pasta is cooking, heat the oil in a large skillet over a medium flame. Add garlic and cook until fragrant, about one minute.

3.) Add the parsley, olives, capers, anchovy paste, oregano and crushed red pepper to the skillet, and sauté for two minutes.

4.) Add the tomatoes and simmer for about five minutes.

5.) Stir in the arugula and cook for one minute more, until the greens begin to wilt.

6.) Drain pasta and add it to the skillet, tossing it with the sauce until coated.

7.) Top with grated cheese and serve.

Caesar Salad
With Homemade Croutons
Serves 4

Ingredients

Homemade Croutons:

> 1 packed cup (240mL) cubed semolina bread (day-old is fine)
>
> 2 cloves of garlic, roughly chopped
>
> 2 tablespoons olive oil

Caesar Salad:

> 4 cloves garlic
>
> 6 tablespoons extra virgin olive oil, divided
>
> Coarse black pepper, to taste

2 tablespoons anchovy paste (optional for vegetarians)

1 teaspoon Worcestershire sauce (6-8 drops)

1 large egg yolk or 1/4 cup pasteurized egg product

Juice of 1 large lemon

2 hearts of romaine lettuce, coarsely chopped

Coarse salt, to taste

Directions

Homemade Croutons:

1.) Heat a small skillet over medium heat. Add olive oil, and garlic.

2.) When the garlic sizzles, add the bread and toast until golden, tossing occasionally, six to eight minutes.

3.) Sprinkle the cubed bread with a little pepper and remove from the heat.

Caesar Salad:

1.) Rub the inside of a large salad bowl with one clove of cracked garlic. Place that clove and a second clove aside. Mince the remaining two cloves and place them in a small bowl.

2.) Combine the minced garlic and about 4 tablespoons olive oil in a small bowl or skillet. Heat the garlic and oil, (either in a microwave oven for one minute, or over low heat on a stovetop, for two to three minutes).

3.) Stir the anchovy paste into the warm olive oil with a fork and let stand until the olive oil returns to room temperature.

4.) Place the Worcestershire sauce and egg yolk or egg product into a salad bowl and stir with a fork.

5.) Stir lemon juice into the egg.

6.) In a slow and steady stream, add the olive oil, garlic and anchovy mixture to the egg and lemon juice, continually whisking with a fork. This is your dressing.

7.) Add the romaine to the bowl and toss with tongs to coat in dressing.

8.) Add a generous amount of cheese and croutons. Season with salt and pepper to taste.

Fish Tacos With Salsa Verde

Serves 4

Ingredients

1 pound halibut or other meaty white fish
   fillets (like Mahi Mahi, Monk fish, or Cod)

Juice of 2 limes

1 6-oz (160g) can of diced green chilies

1 teaspoon crushed red pepper flakes

1 12-ounce (340g) can whole tomatillos,
   drained

1/4 cup chopped cilantro

2 1/2 teaspoons coarse salt, plus more to taste

8 6-inch (15cm) corn tortillas

2 tablespoons chili powder

1/4 teaspoon cayenne pepper, or to taste

1 tablespoon extra-virgin olive oil

1 avocado, peeled and thinly sliced

Directions

1.) Preheat the oven to 225°F (107°C).

2.) Place the fish in a medium bowl and drizzle with half of the lime juice. Cover and refrigerate for fifteen minutes.

3.) Squeeze juice and flesh from the tomatillos with hands, into a medium bowl. Throw away the skins. Mash the tomatillos with a fork.

4.) Add green chilies, remaining lime juice, cilantro, red pepper flakes, and 2 teaspoons salt to tomatillos and mix well. This is your salsa.

5.) Spread the tortillas on baking sheet and warm in the oven for about 10 minutes.

6.) In a small bowl, combine the chili powder, cayenne pepper and 1/2 teaspoon of the salt. Remove the fish from the lime juice, pat dry and cover with the spice rub.

7.) In a large, nonstick skillet, heat the olive oil and cook fish over medium heat, about four minutes on each side.

8.) Break the fish into bite-size pieces and season to taste with salt and pepper.

9.) Lay out fish nuggets in tortillas and top with salsa and avocado slices. Garnish with cilantro if desired.

SELECTED RESOURCES BY
RACHAEL RAY

Books

Ray, Rachael. *Rachael Ray 2,4,6,8 Great Meals for Couples or Crowds*. (New York: Clarkson Potter, 2006.)

Ray, Rachael. *Rachael Ray's 30-Minute Meals Comfort Foods*, (New York: Lake Isle Press, 2000.)

Ray, Rachael. *Rachael Ray's More Than 300 Recipes to Cook Every Day: Book of 10*. (New York: Clarkson Potter, 2009.)

Ray, Rachael. *Week in a Day: Five Dishes • One Day*. (New York City: Atria, Simon & Schuster, 2013.)

Ray, Rachael. *Yum-O! The Family Cookbook*, (New York: Clarkson Potter, 2008.)

Websites

foodnetwork.com

rachaelray.com

yum-o.org

CHRONOLOGY

1968 — Rachael Domenic Ray is born on August 25,1976. The Ray family moves to Lake Luzerne, New York.

1981 — James and Elsa Ray divorce.

1986 — Ray graduates from high school.

1986-1988 — Attends Pace University.

1991 — Lands at candy counter at Macy's; soon promoted to fresh foods manager.

1993 — Becomes the store manager and buyer at Agata & Valentina, gourmet food shop in New York City.

1994 — Robbed at gunpoint.

1995 — Become food buyer for Cowan & Lobel in Albany.

1996 — Begins in-store demonstrations of how to make 30-Minute Meals at Cowan & Lovel.

1997-2001 — Tapes weekly 30-Minute Meal segments on WRGB news in Albany.

1998 — Publishes first book of recipes—*30 Minute Meals.*

2001 — Appears on *Today Show.*

2001 — Signs with Food Network.

2001 — *30-Minute Meals* TV show debuts.

2002 — *$40 a Day* premieres.

2004 — Signs multi-million dollar book deal with Clarkson Potter.

2005 — Marries John Cusimano.

2005 — First issue of *Every Day With Rachael Ray* comes out.

2006 — Time Magazine calls her one of the 100 People Who Shape Our World.

2006 — *Rachael Ray* daytime talk show premieres.

2007 — Starts Yum-O Organization to help children's eating habits.

2008 — Wins Emmy for her daytime talk show.

2009 — Wins 2nd Emmy for her daytime talk show.

2010 — *Week in a Day* TV show premieres.

2012 — *Rachael Vs. Guy* debuts.

CHAPTER NOTES

Chapter 1: Small-Town Values, Big Work Ethic

1. Carr, David, "Rachael Ray Gives the Gift of Time," The *New York Times*, October 23, 2006, http://www.nytimes.com/2006/10/23/business/media/23carr.html?_r=0
2. "Rachael Ray Biography," *People*, http://www.people.com/people/rachael_ray/biography/
3. Ray, Rachael, *Rachael Ray's 30-Minute Meals Comfort Foods*, (New York: Lake Isle Press, 2000.)
4. Kaufman, Joanne, "Rachael Ray's Recipe for Joy," *Good Housekeeping*, August 2006, http://connection.ebscohost.com/c/articles/22316399/rachael-rays-recipe-joy
5. Jacobs, Laura, "Just Say Yum-O!" *Vanity Fair*, October 2007, http://www.vanityfair.com/culture/2007/10/rachaelray200710
6. "Rachael Ray," *Budget Travel*, August 1, 2005, http://www.budgettravel.com/feature/0509_WindoworAisle_RachaelRay,3767/
7. Keeps, David, "Rachael Ray's Rules for a Delicious Life." *Good Housekeeping*, May 28, 2010, http://www.goodhousekeeping.com/life/inspirational-stories/interviews/a18866/rachael-ray-biography/
8. "Rachael Ray: *Chefography*," (Episode: CHSP09) Food Network, 2007, http://www.foodnetwork.com/shows/food-network-specials/all-specials/rachael-ray.html
9. Schawbel, Dan, "Rachael Ray: What You Can Learn From Her Rise To Fame," *Forbes*, December 3, 2013, http://www.forbes.com/sites/danschawbel/2013/12/03/rachael-ray-what-you-can-learn-from-her-rise-to-fame/
10. Ray, Rachael, "A Note from Rachael: I Love You, Mom!" April 7, 2015, http://www.rachaelray.com/2015/04/rachael-ray-may-letter
11. Kaufman, Joanne, "Rachael Ray's Recipe for Joy,"
12. Chi, Paul, "Rachael Ray: 'I Sat Alone' in the Cafeteria," *People*. December 7, 2007, http://www.people.com/people/article/0,,20164849,00.html
13. Ray, Rachael, "A Note from Rachael: I Love You, Mom!"

14. "Who Knew!" *Every Day With Rachael Ray*, http://www.rachaelray mag.com/rachael-ray/ask-rachael-ray/rach-trivia-qa

15. Abrams, Dennis, *Rachael Ray: Food Entrepreneur*, (New York: Chelsea House Publishing, 2009.)

16. Kaufman, Joanne, "Rachael Ray's Recipe for Joy."

17. "Who Knew!" *Every Day With Rachael Ray*, http://www.rachaelray mag.com/rachael-ray/ask-rachael-ray/rach-trivia-qa

18. "Rachael Goes Back to High School," The *Rachael Ray Show*, August 27, 2007, http://www.rachaelrayshow.com/tips/12374_ Rachael_Goes_Back_to_High_School/

19. "The True Story of Rachael Ray," *Food Network Musings*, May 11, 2007, http://foodnetworkmusings.blogspot.com/2007/05/true-story-of-rachael-ray.html

20. Abrams, Dennis, *Rachael Ray: Food Entrepreneur*, (New York: Chelsea House Publishing, 2009.)

Chapter 2: **To the City and Back**

1. Jacobs, Laura, "Just Say Yum-O!" *Vanity Fair*, October 2007, http://www.vanityfair.com/culture/2007/10/rachaelray200710

2. "Rach's Faves," *Every Day With Rachael Ray,* http://www. rachaelraymag.com/rachael-ray/ask-rachael-ray/rachs-faves-qa

3. Salkin, Allen, *From Scratch: Inside the Food Network*, (New York: G.P. Putnam's Sons, 2013.)

4. "Rachael Revisits Her Past With TV Guide," *TV Guide*, December 21, 2006, http://www.everythingrachaelray.com/2006/12/rachael-revisits-her-past-with-tv-guide.html

5. "Rachael Ray Biography." *People*, http://www.people.com/people/ rachael_ray/biography/

6. Jacobs, Laura, "Just Say Yum-O!"

Chapter 3: **Heading Home to Success**

1. Keeps, David, "Rachael Ray's Rules for a Delicious Life" *Good Housekeeping*, May 28, 2010, http://www.goodhousekeeping.com/ life/inspirational-stories/interviews/a18866/rachael-ray-biography/

2. Ibid.
3. Jacobs, Laura, "Just Say Yum-O!" *Vanity Fair*, October, 2007, http://www.vanityfair.com/culture/2007/10/rachaelray200710
4. Keel, Beverly, "Rachael Ray's Recipe for Success," *American Profile*, October 9, 2005, http://americanprofile.com/articles/rachael-rays-recipe-for-success/
5. Newsweek Staff, "Women Leaders' Success Secrets." *Newsweek*, October 9, 2007, http://www.newsweek.com/women-leaders-success-secrets-103451
6. Keeps, David, "Rachael Ray's Rules for a Delicious Life," *Good Housekeeping*, May 28, 2010, http://www.goodhousekeeping.com/life/inspirational-stories/interviews/a18866/rachael-ray-biography/
7. Ray, Rachael, *30-Minute Meals*, (New York: Lake Isle Press, 1999.)
8. Newsweek Staff, "Women Leaders' Success Secrets."
9. Ray, Rachael, *Just in Time*, (New York: Clarkson Potter, 2007.)
10. Batali, Mario, "The 2006 Time 100: Rachael Ray," *Time*, May 8, 2006, http://content.time.com/time/specials/packages/article/0,28804,1975813_1975838_1976219,00.html

Chapter 4: The Perfect Storm

1. Clewley, Chandra, "The Next Food Network Star Season 6: Exclusive Interview with Bob Tuschman," *Reality Wanted*, June 8, 2010, http://www.realitywanted.com/newsitem/3340-the-next-food-network-star-season-6-exclusive-interview-with-bob-tuschman#.VaVgF0Vl-8V
2. "That Time Rachael Hung Up on the 'TODAY' Show," The *Rachael Ray Show*, November 24, 2014, http://www.rachaelrayshow.com/celebs/19194_cat_deeley_puts_rach_on_the_spot/
3. Jacobs, Laura, "Just Say Yum-O!" *Vanity Fair*, October 2007, http://www.vanityfair.com/culture/2007/10/rachaelray200710
4. Ibid.
5. Severson, Kim, "Being Rachael Ray: How Cool Is That?" The *New York Times*, October 19, 2005, http://www.nytimes.com/2005/10/19/dining/being-rachael-ray-how-cool-is-that.html

Chapter 5: America Discovers Rachael Ray

1. Long, Sarah, "10 Things You Didn't Know About Rachael Ray," September 11, 2014, http://www.sheknows.com/entertainment/articles/1049913/things-you-didnt-know-about-rachael-ray.
2. Salkin, Allen, *From Scratch: Inside the Food Network*, (New York: G.P. Putnam's Sons, 2013.)
3. Grimes, William, "I'm Cooking As Fast As I Can," The *New York Times*, September 15, 2004. http://www.nytimes.com/2004/09/15/dining/15FAST.html
4. Jill Pellettieri, "Rachael Ray: Why Food Snobs Should Stop Picking On Her," *Slate*, July 13, 2005. http://www.slate.com/articles/life/food/2005/07/rachael_ray.html

Chapter 6: Making Time for a Personal Life

1. "Rachael Ray Biography," *People*. http://www.people.com/people/rachael_ray/biography/
2. "Rachael Ray: On the Rocks!" *People*, January 30, 2008, http://www.people.com/people/article/0,,20424310,00.html
3. *Larry King Live!* CNN, December 25, 2006, http://www.cnn.com/TRANSCRIPTS/0612/25/lkl.09.html
4. Hamm, Liza and Tauber, Michelle, "Rachael Ray's Recipe for Marriage," *People,* May 2, 2007, http://www.people.com/people/article/0,,20037511,00.html
5. *Larry King Live!* CNN.
6. Moore, Arden. "Rachael Ray Dishes It Out on Oh Behave!—How Cool Is That," *Pet Life Radio*, http://www.petliferadio.com/behaveep64.html

Chapter 8: The Oprah of Cooking

1. *Larry King Live!* CNN, December 25, 2006. http://www.cnn.com/TRANSCRIPTS/0612/25/lkl.09.html
2. *Larry King Live!* CNN
3. Ray, Rachael, *Rachael Ray's Book of 10*, (New York, NY: Clarkson Potter, 2009.)

4. Schawbel, Dan, "Rachael Ray: What You Can Learn From Her Rise To Fame," *Forbes*, December 3, 2013, http://www.forbes.com/sites/danschawbel/2013/12/03/rachael-ray-what-you-can-learn-from-her-rise-to-fame/

5. McFadden, Cynthia and Rosenberg, Sarah, "Rachael Ray: 'I Don't Regret a Thing,'" *ABC News*. March 2, 2009, http://abcnews.go.com/Nightline/Recipes/rachael-ray-regret-thing/story?id=6976299

6. Ray, Rachael, *Yum-O! The Family Cookbook*, (New York: Clarkson Potter, 2008.)

7. Schawbel, Dan, "Rachael Ray: What You Can Learn From Her Rise To Fame."

cannellini—A white Italian kidney bean.

capers—A type of pickled flower bud from a shrub like bush.

caponata—A Sicilian dish of eggplant with celery and sweetened vinegar.

carbonara—A pasta dish from Rome with eggs, cheese, bacon, and black pepper.

caviar—The pickled roe (fish eggs) of a large fish, often a sturgeon; usually a high-end delicacy.

charisma—A personal magnetism that attracts other people.

gelato—Italian ice cream.

jambalaya—Spicy Louisiana dish of rice cooked with ham, sausage, chicken or shellfish, herbs and spices, as well as tomatoes, onions, celery, and peppers.

maque choux (mock-choo)—Classic Cajun or Creole dish of stewed corn and vegetables.

parmigiano-reggiano—Hard, granular cheese that is often grated on top of pasta.

pâté (pah-te)—Mixture of cooked ground meat and fat mixed into a spreadable paste.

prosciutto (pro-shoot-o)—Italian ham cured by drying and typically served in very thin slices.

puttanesca (put-a-nes-ka)—Tangy and salty Italian pasta dish typically featuring tomatoes, olive oil, olives, capers and garlic.

rapini—Broccoli rabe, a bitter-flavored green.

ricotta—Soft, white, unsalted Italian cheese that looks like cottage cheese.

tilapia—African freshwater fish that is now widely sold in supermarkets.

FURTHER READING

Books

Locricchio, Matthew. *Teen Cuisine*. Seattle, WA: Skyscape, 2014.

Marchive, Laurane. *The Green Teen Cookbook*. San Francisco, CA: Zest Books, 2014.

Mendocino Press. *The Cookbook for Teens*. Mendocino, California: Mendocino Press, 2014.

Salkin, Allen. *From Scratch: Inside the Food Network*. New York, NY: G.P. Putnam's Sons, 2013.

Websites

Cooking Teens
cookingteens.com
> *Healthy and tasty recipes for young chefs, as well as articles on young people involved with cooking.*

Teen Recipes
teen-recipes.com
> *A wealth of delicious and simple recipes that teens can prepare.*

Movies

Chef. directed by Jon Favreau. 2014.

The Hundred-Foot Journey. by Lasse Hallström. 2014.

INDEX